THE INTROVERTED POST
BOOK OF MAIL ART
VOL. 6
PO BOX 132
BATH, OHIO 44210 USA

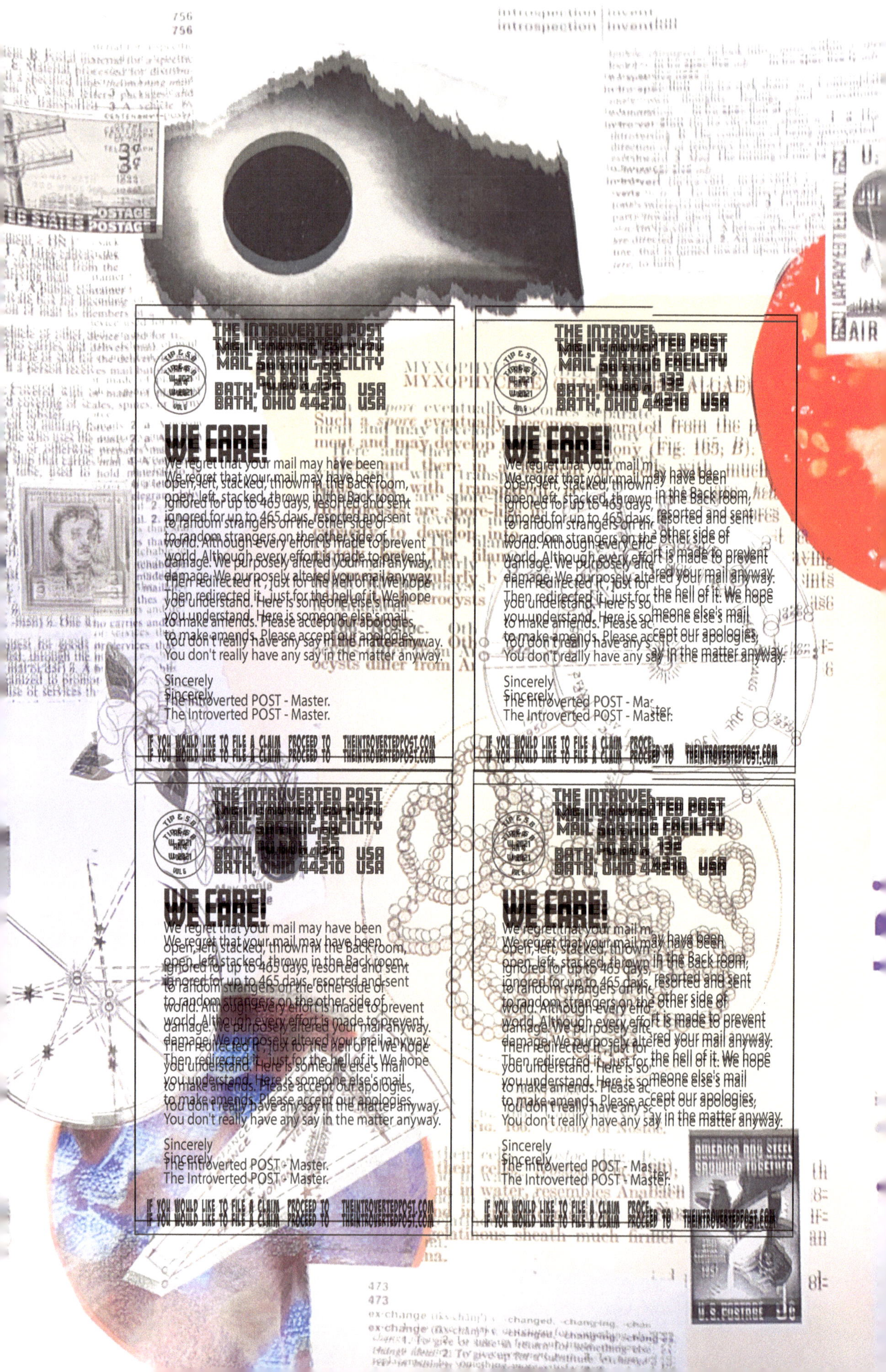

THE INTROVERTED POST
MAIL SORTING FACILITY
BATH, OHIO 44210 USA

WE CARE!

We regret that your mail may have been opened, left, stacked, thrown in the back room, ignored for up to 465 days, resorted and sent to random strangers on the other side of the world. Although every effort is made to prevent damage, We purposely altered your mail anyway. Then redirected it, just for the hell of it. We hope you understand. Here is someone else's mail to make amends. Please accept our apologies, you don't really have any say in the matter anyway.

Sincerely
The Introverted POST - Master.

IF YOU WOULD LIKE TO FILE A CLAIM PROCEED TO THEINTROVERTEDPOST.COM

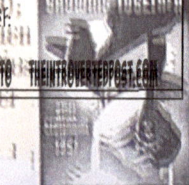

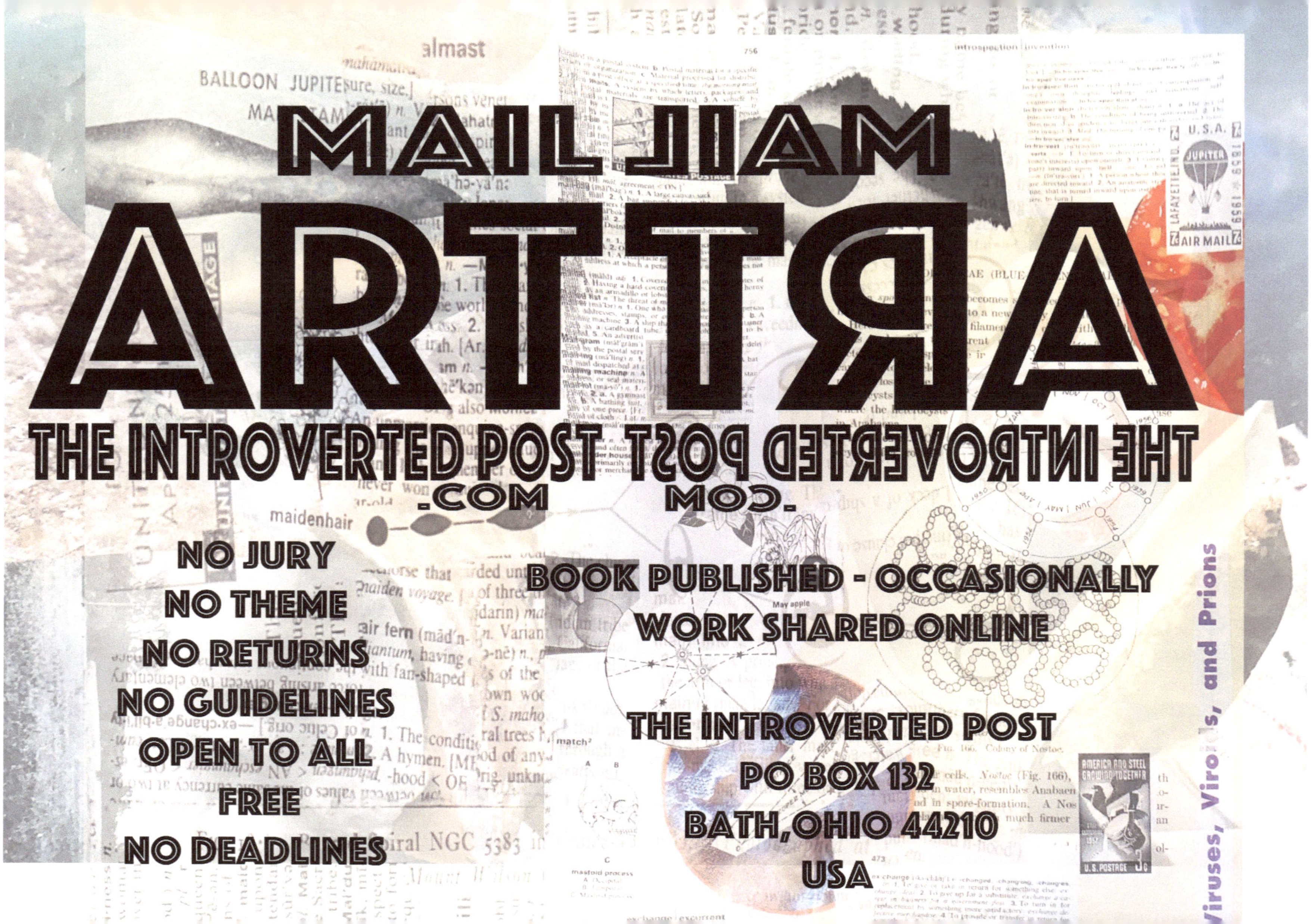

MAIL ARTIST

THE INTROVERTED POST

THE INTROVERTED POST .COM

- BOOK PUBLISHED - OCCASIONALLY WORK SHARED ONLINE

THE INTROVERTED POST
PO BOX 132
BATH, OHIO 44210
USA

- NO JURY
- NO THEME
- NO RETURNS
- NO GUIDELINES
- OPEN TO ALL
- FREE
- NO DEADLINES

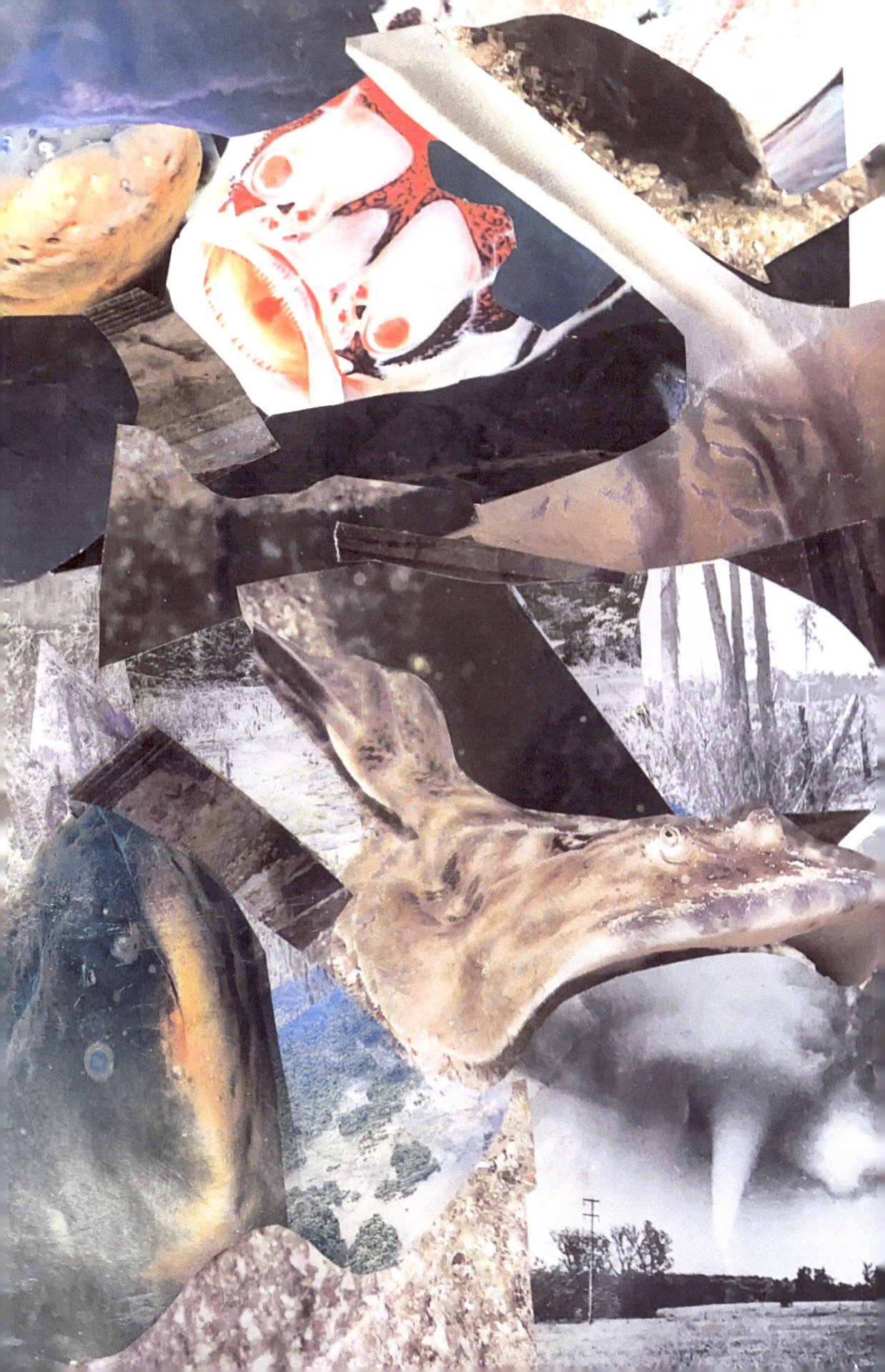

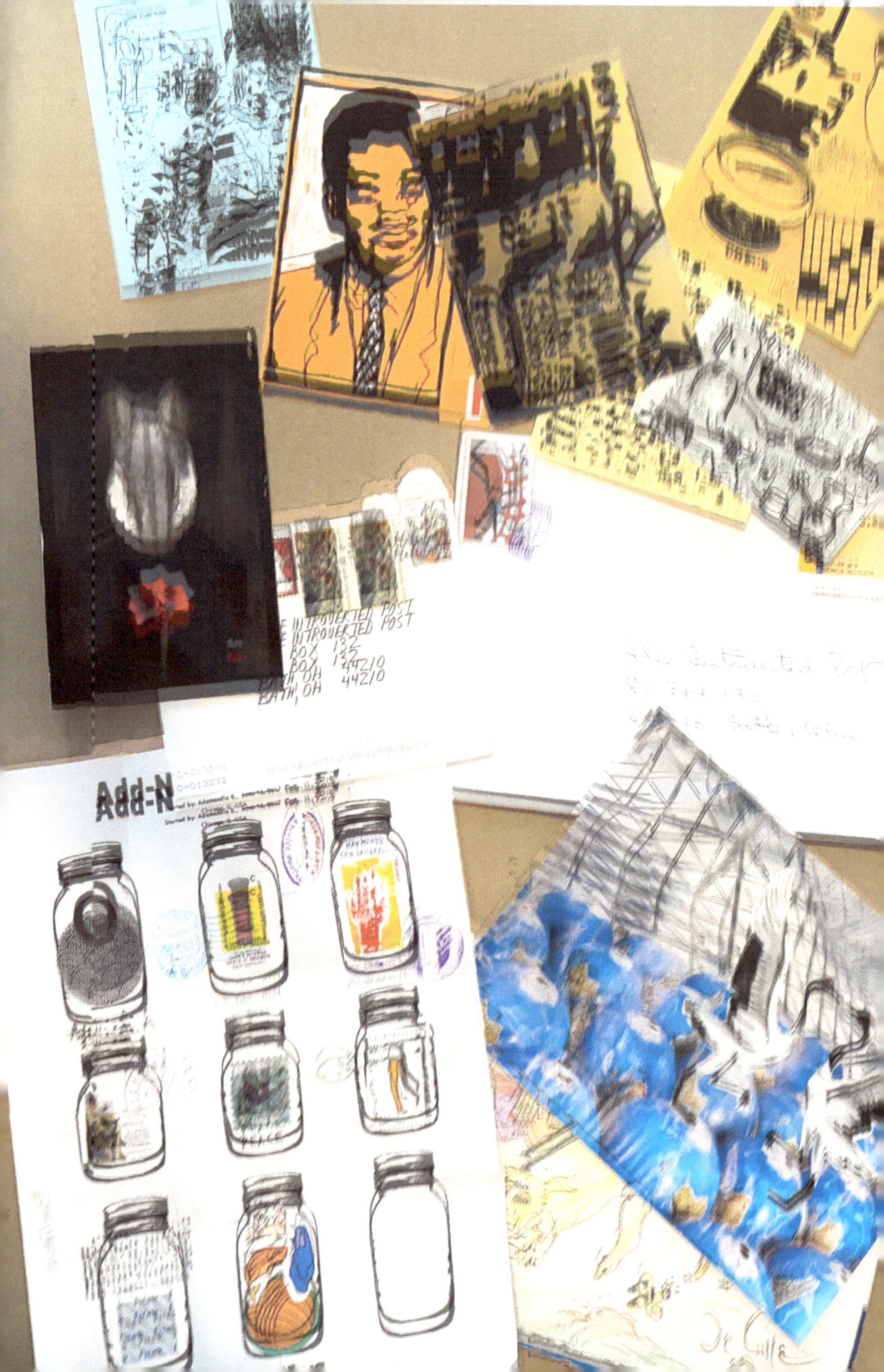

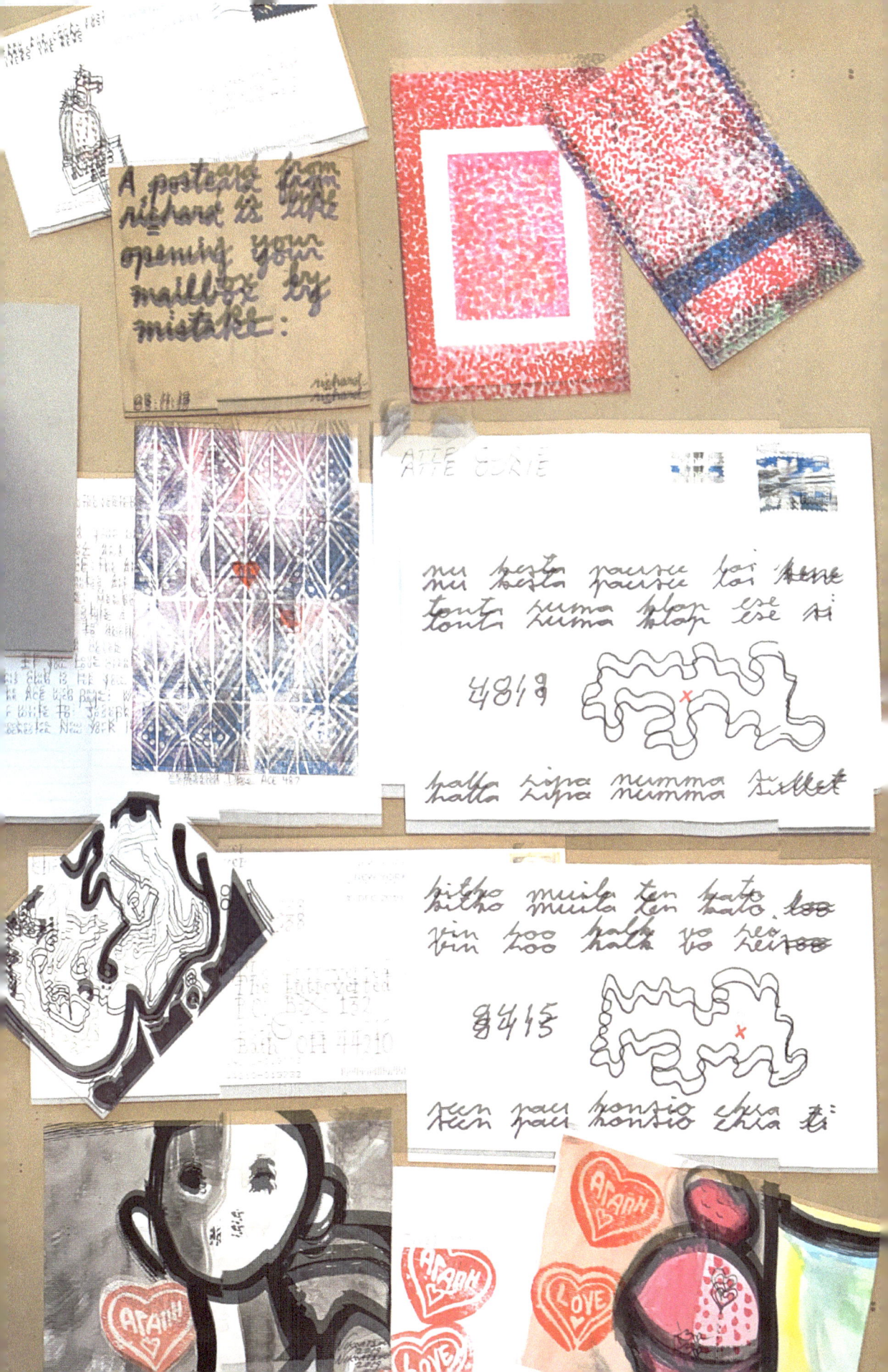

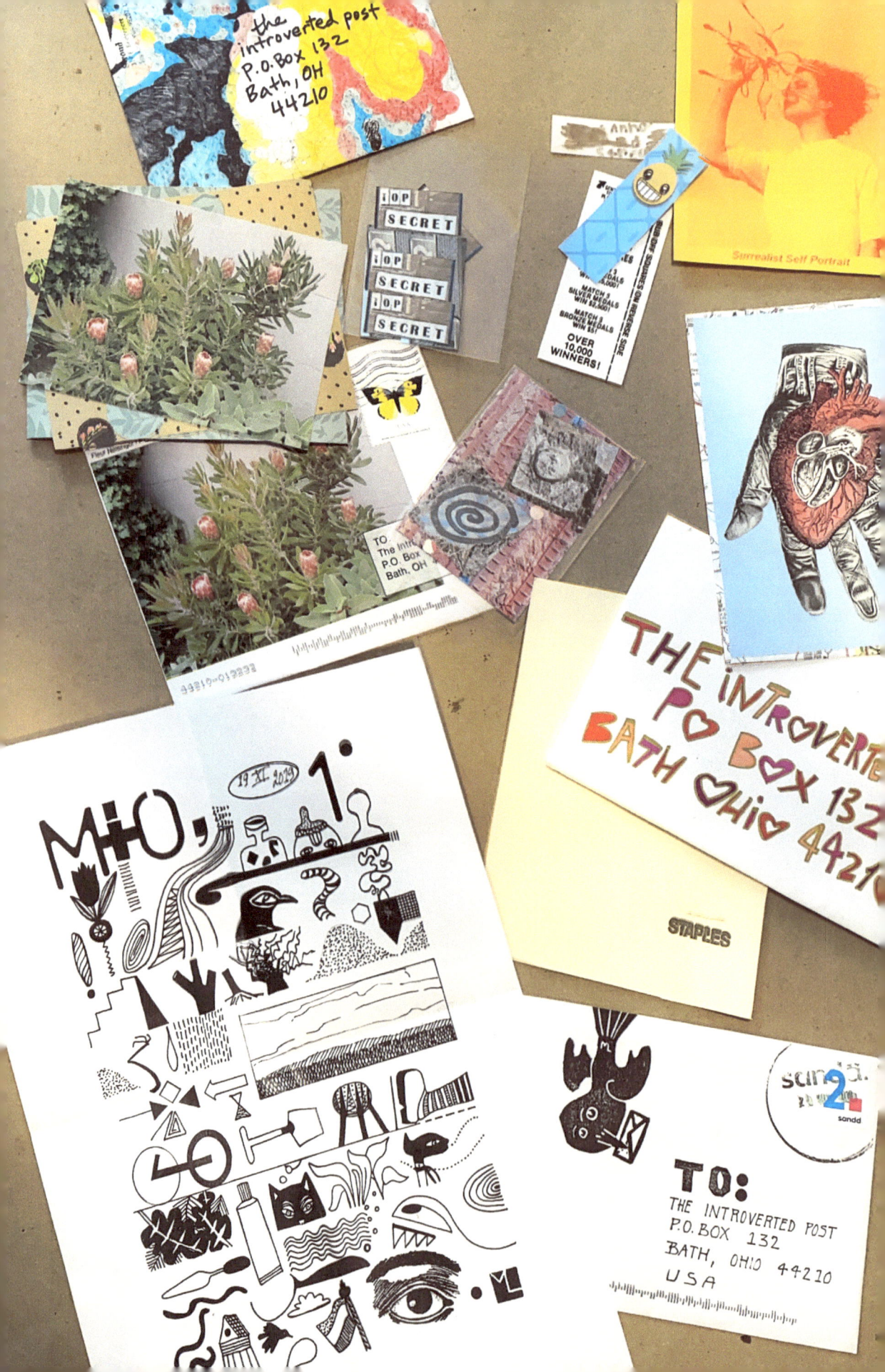

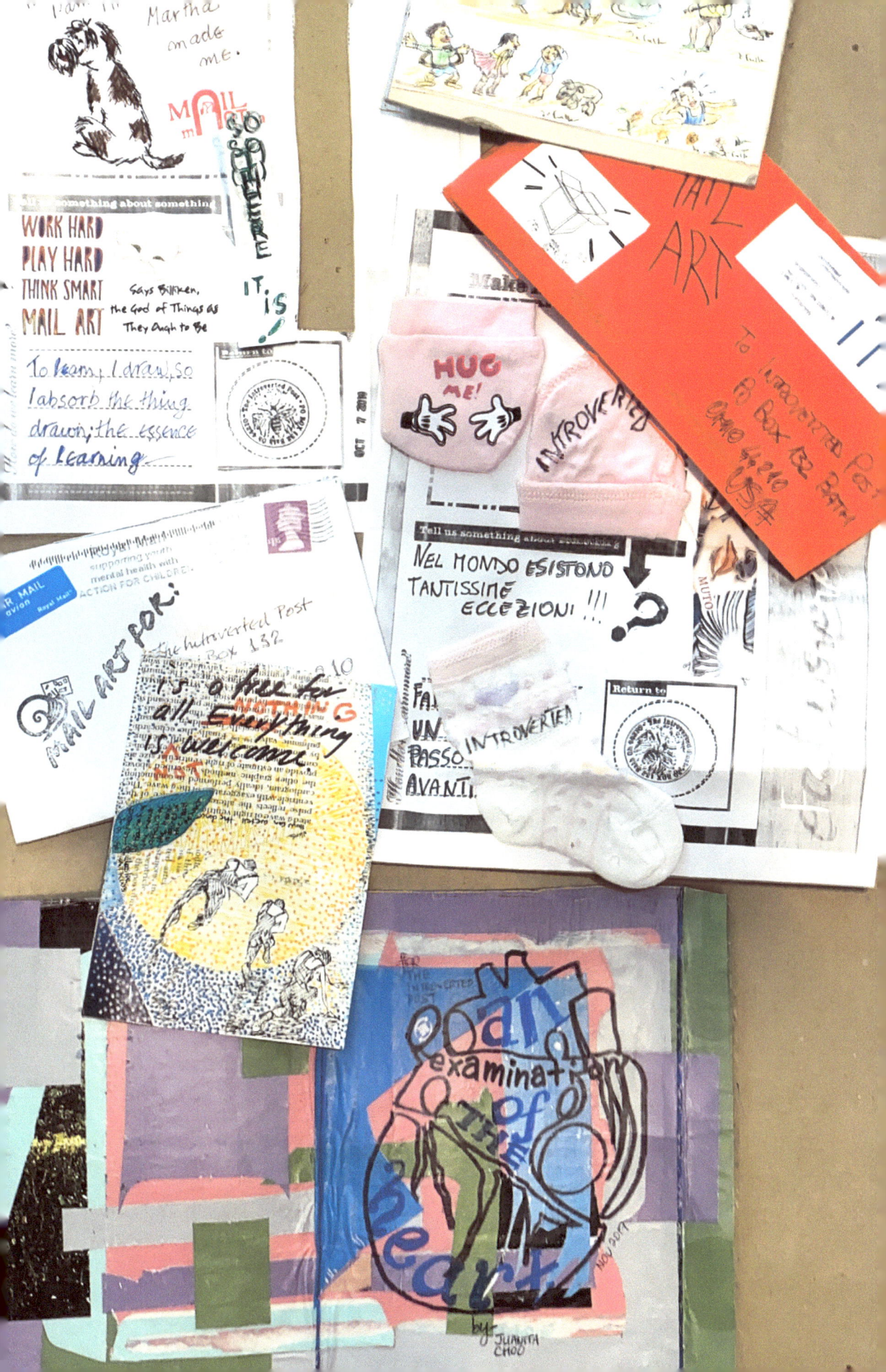

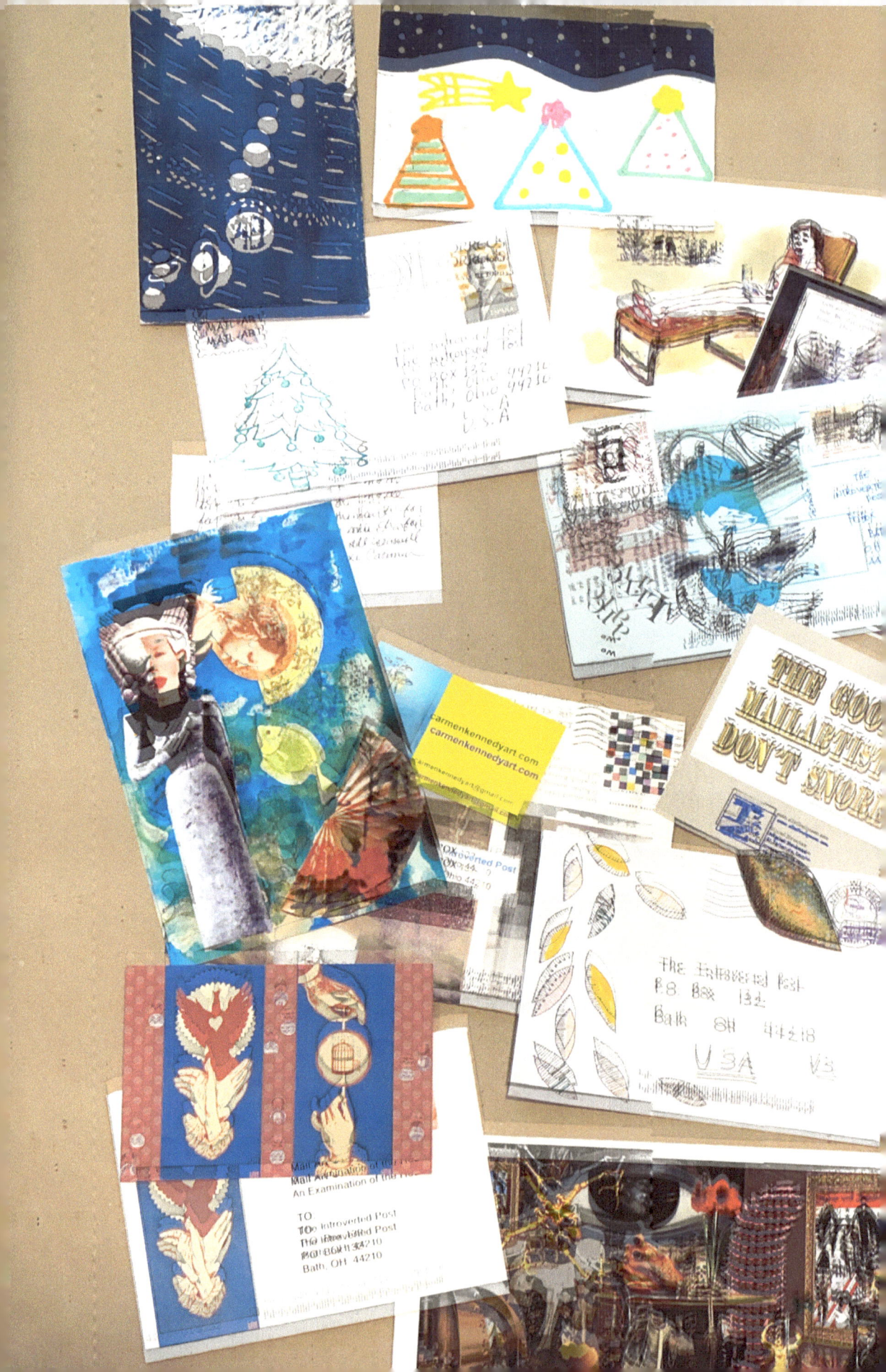

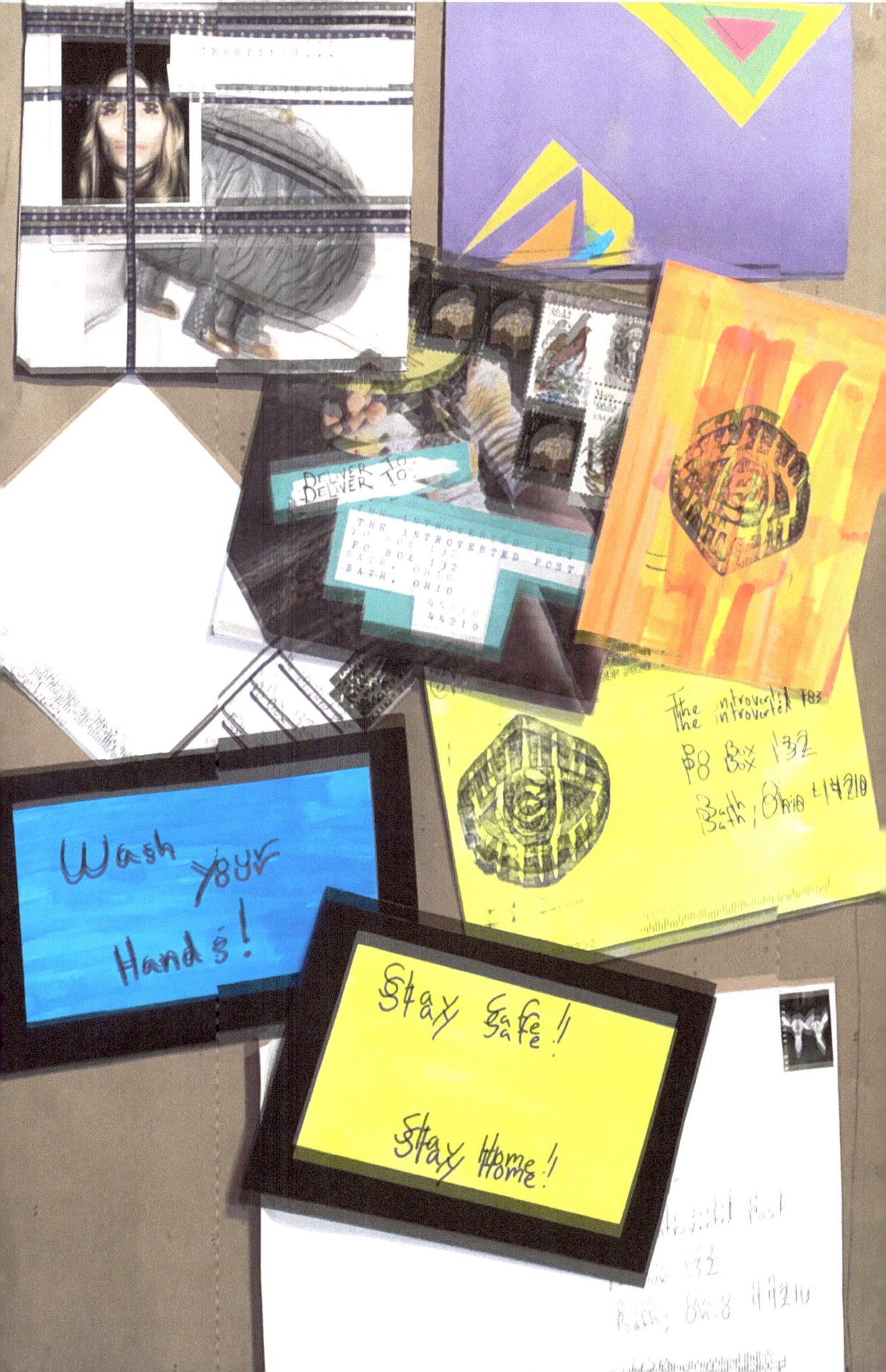

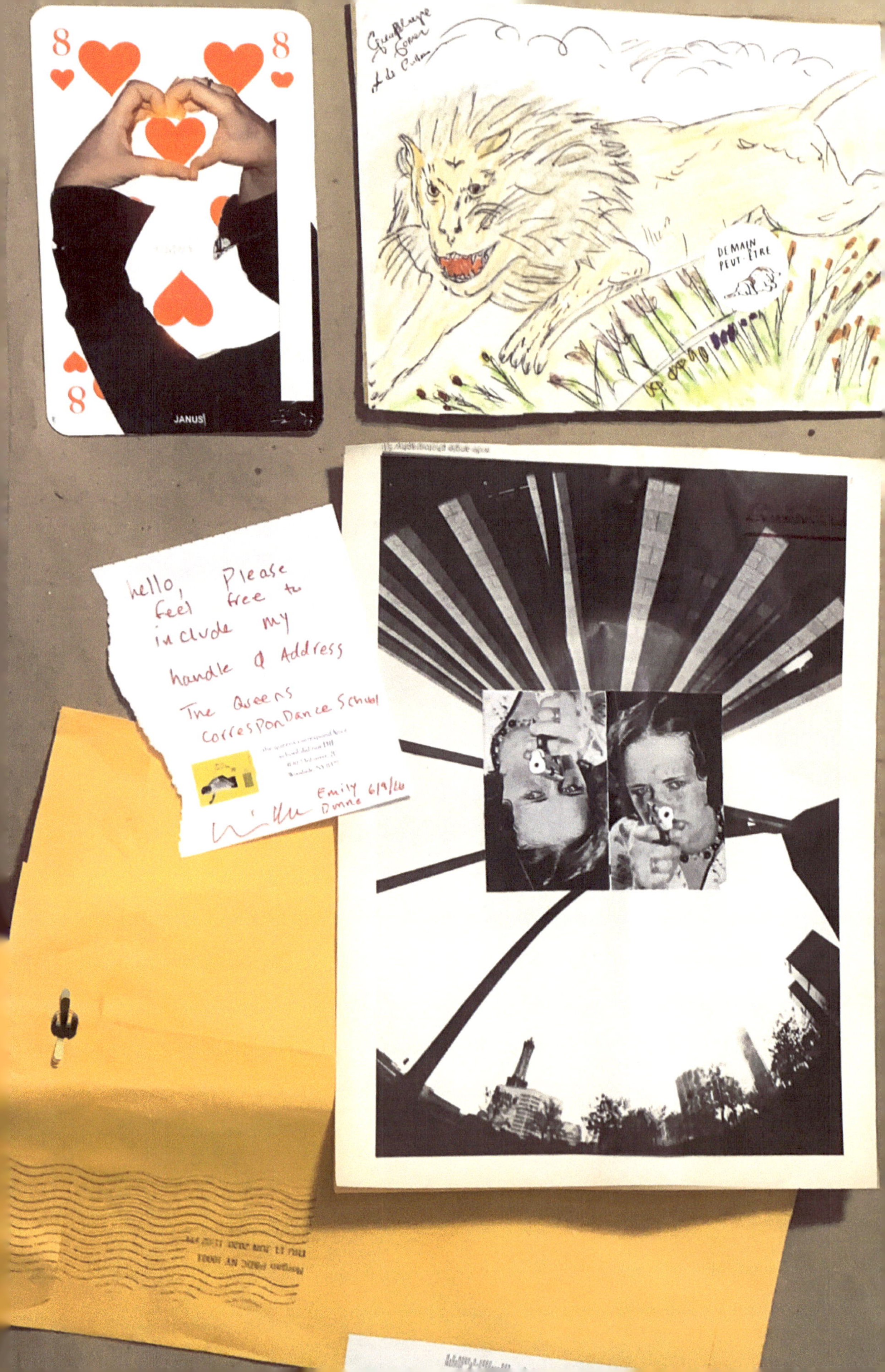

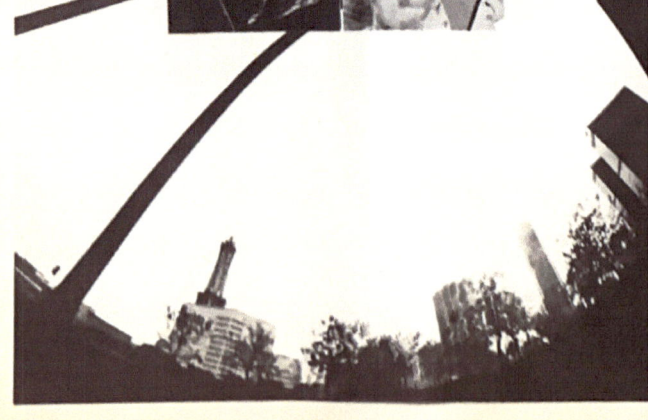

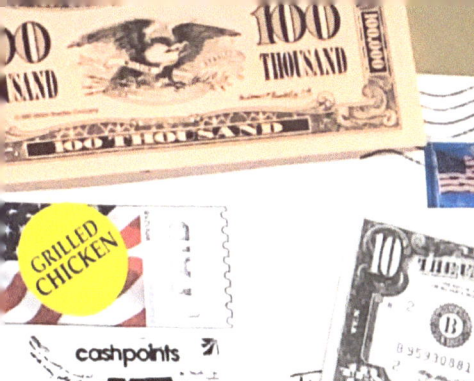
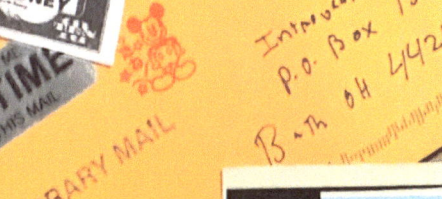
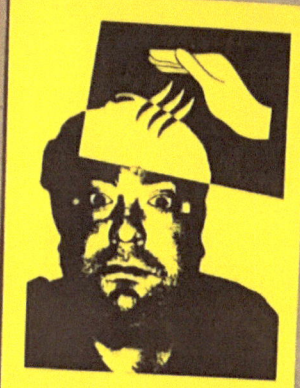
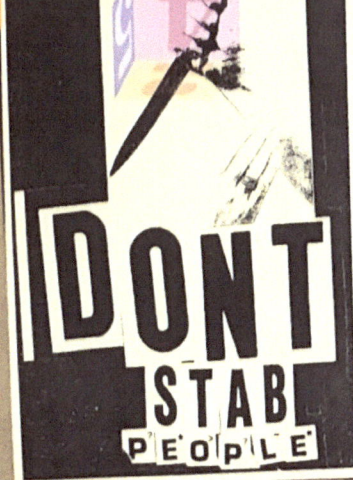
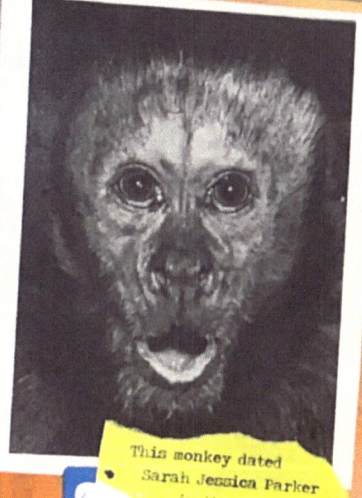
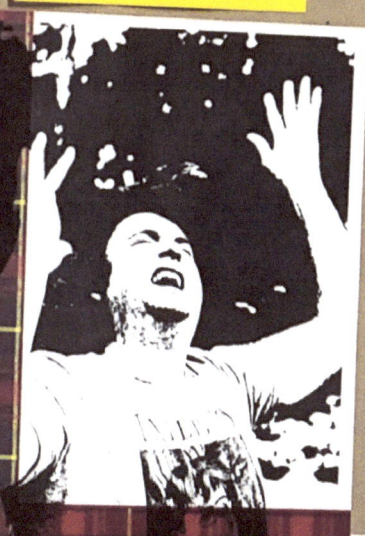
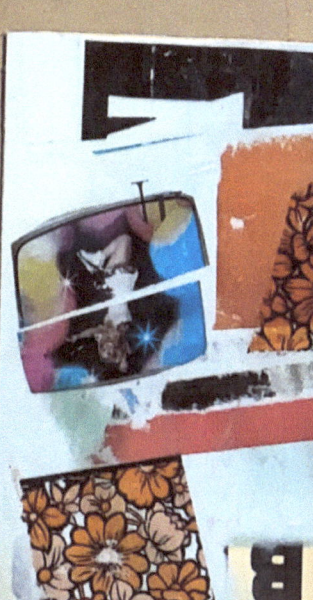

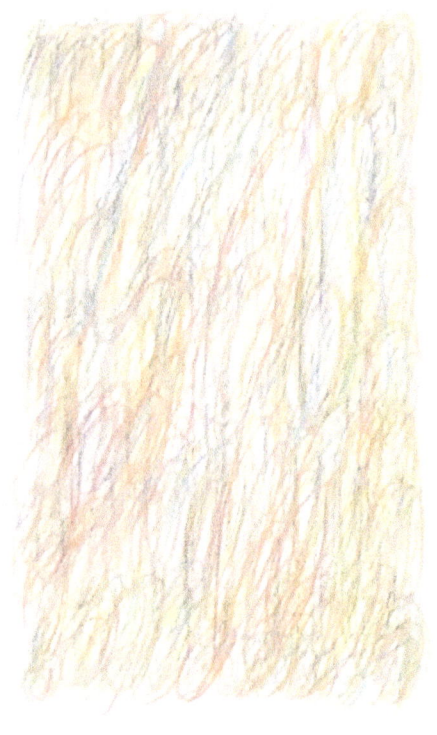
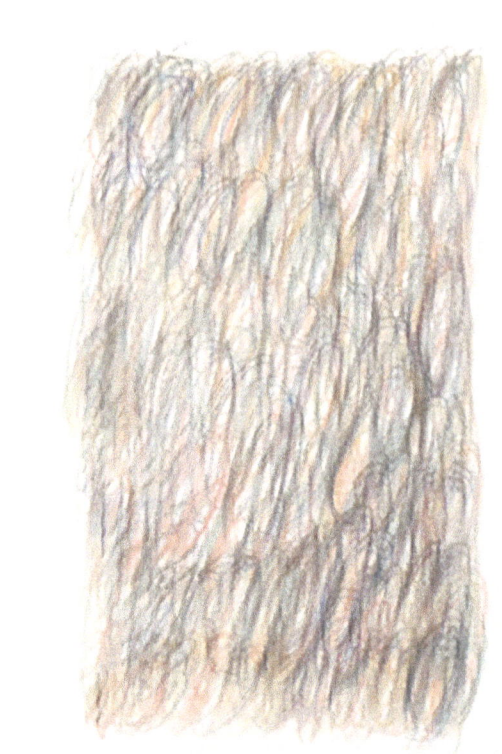

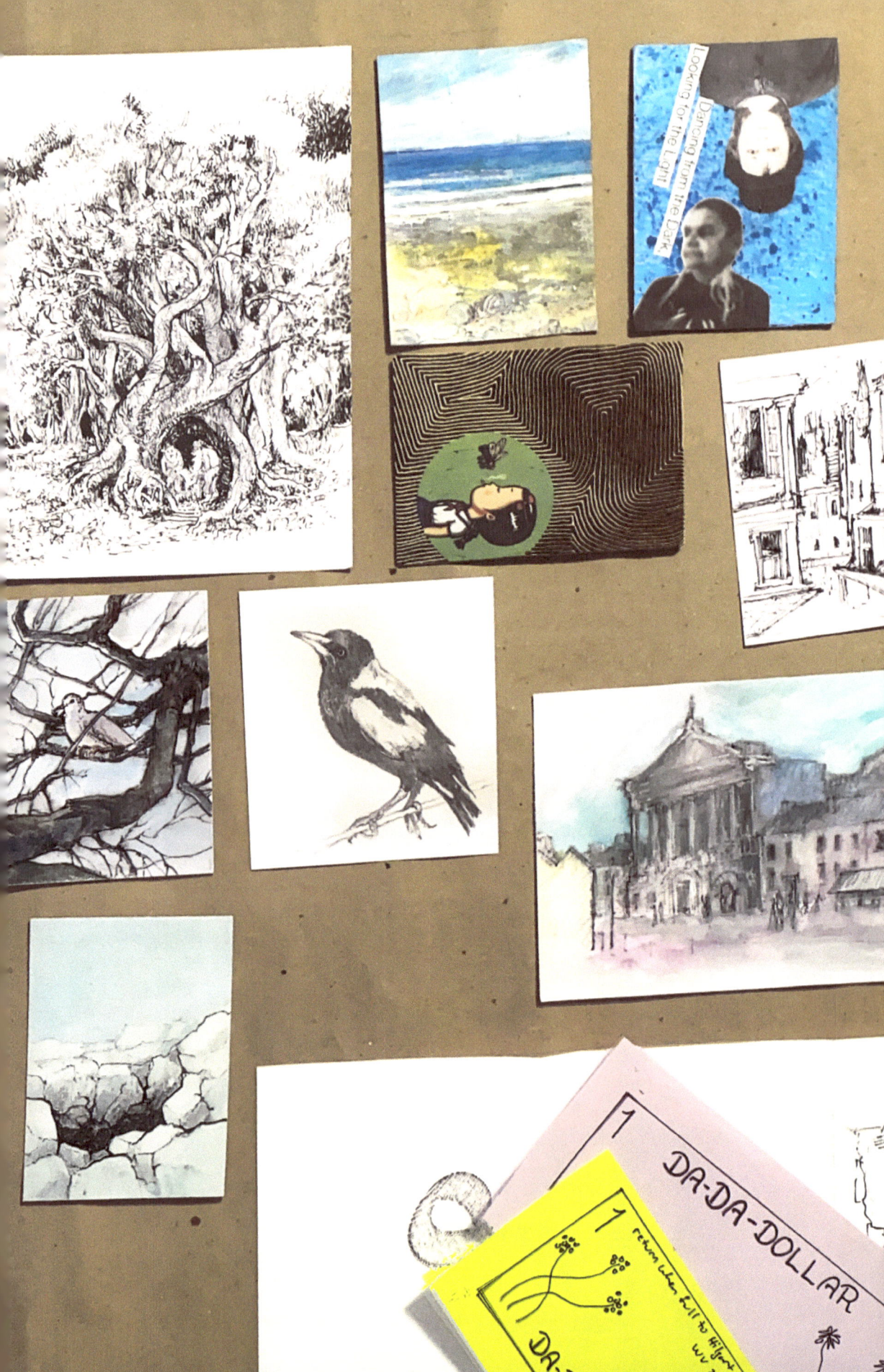

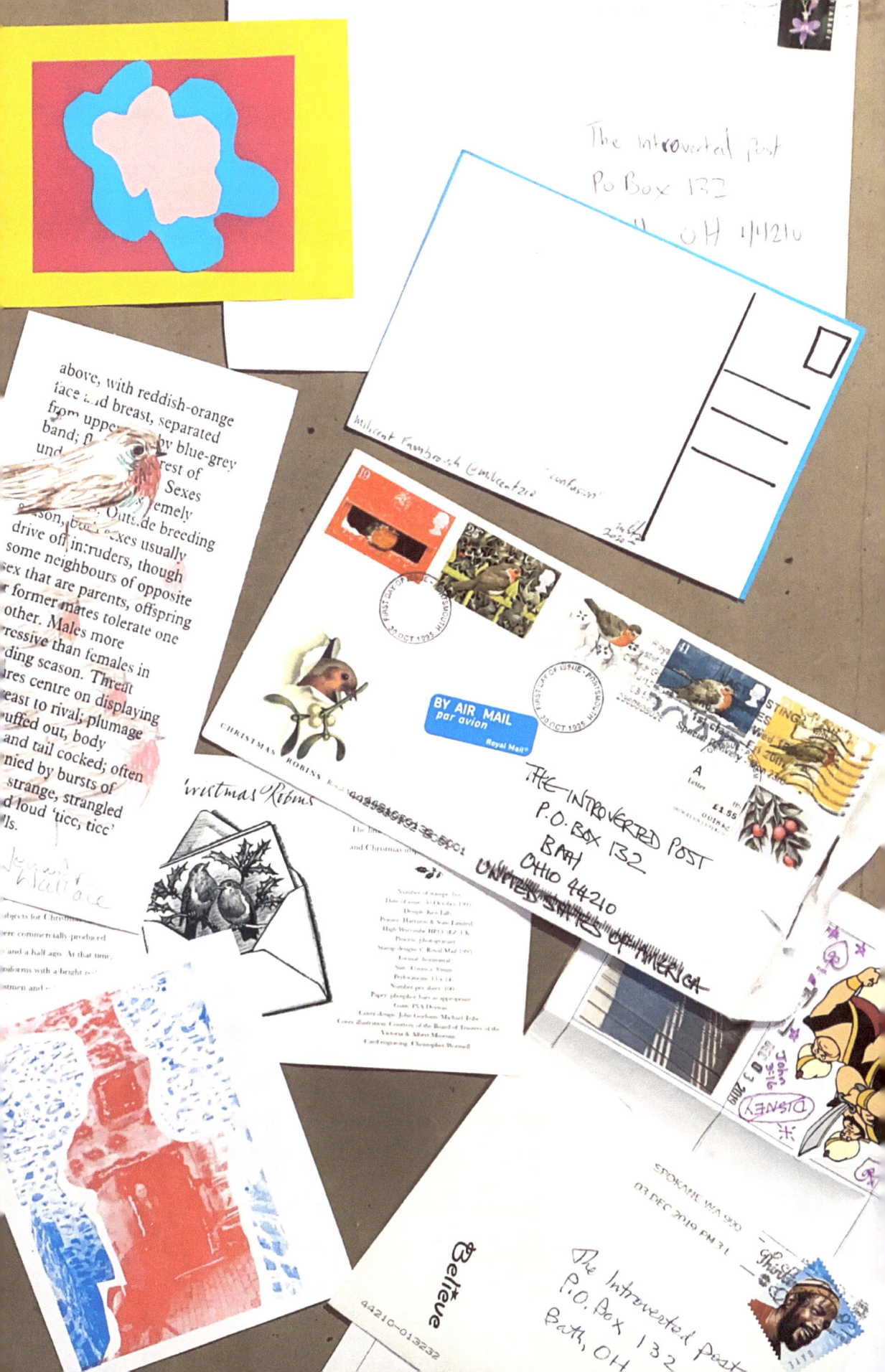

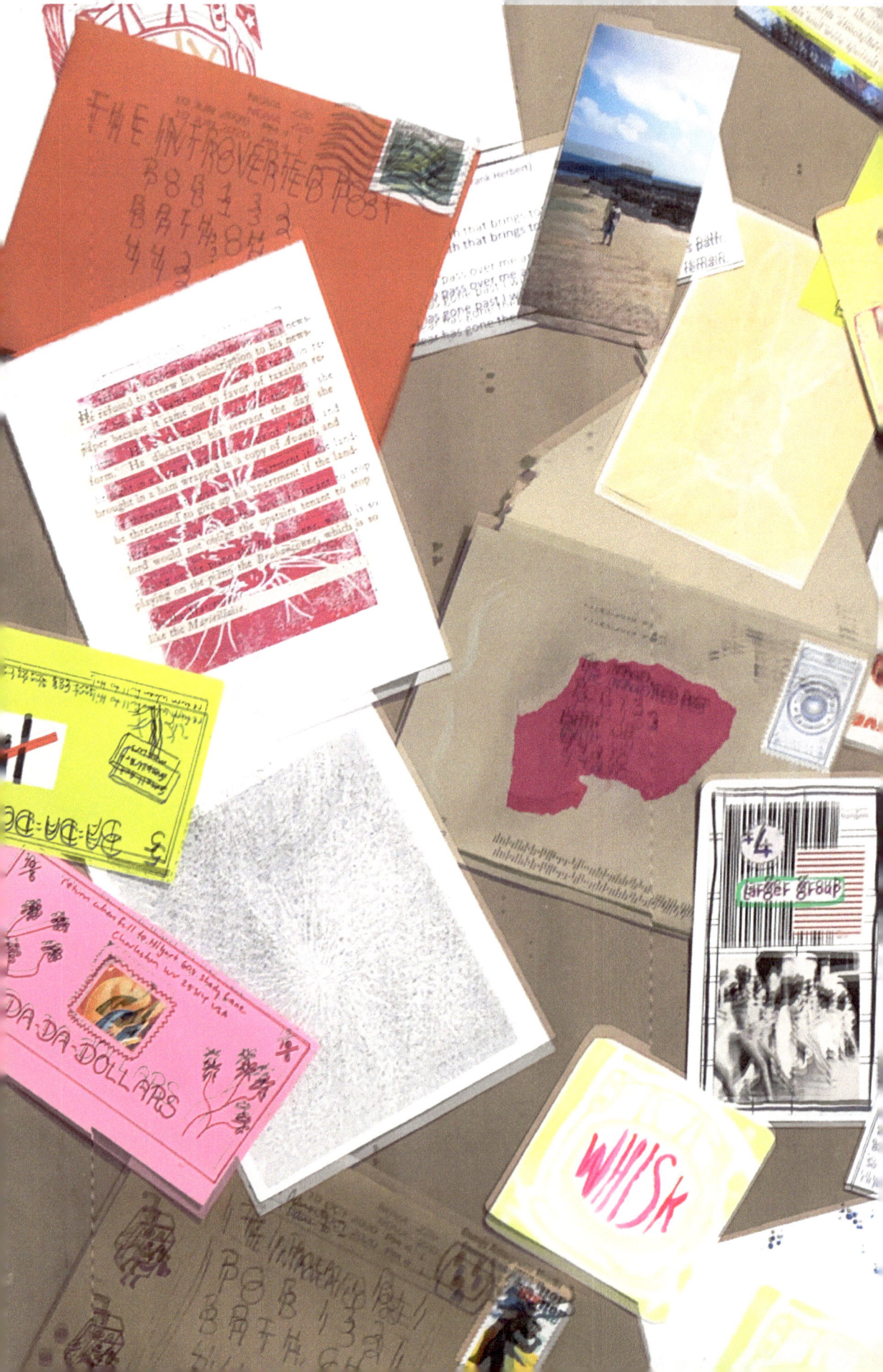

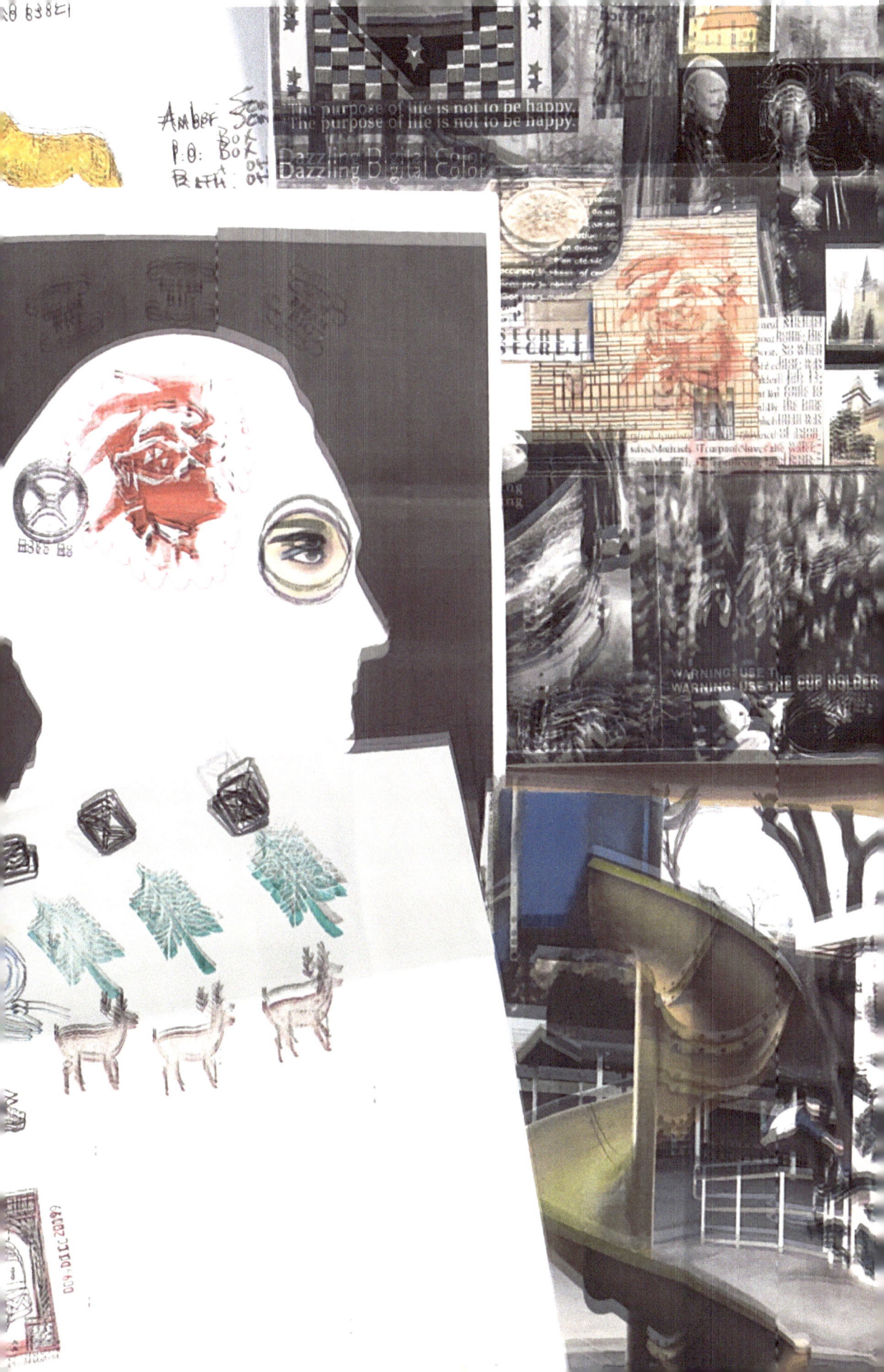

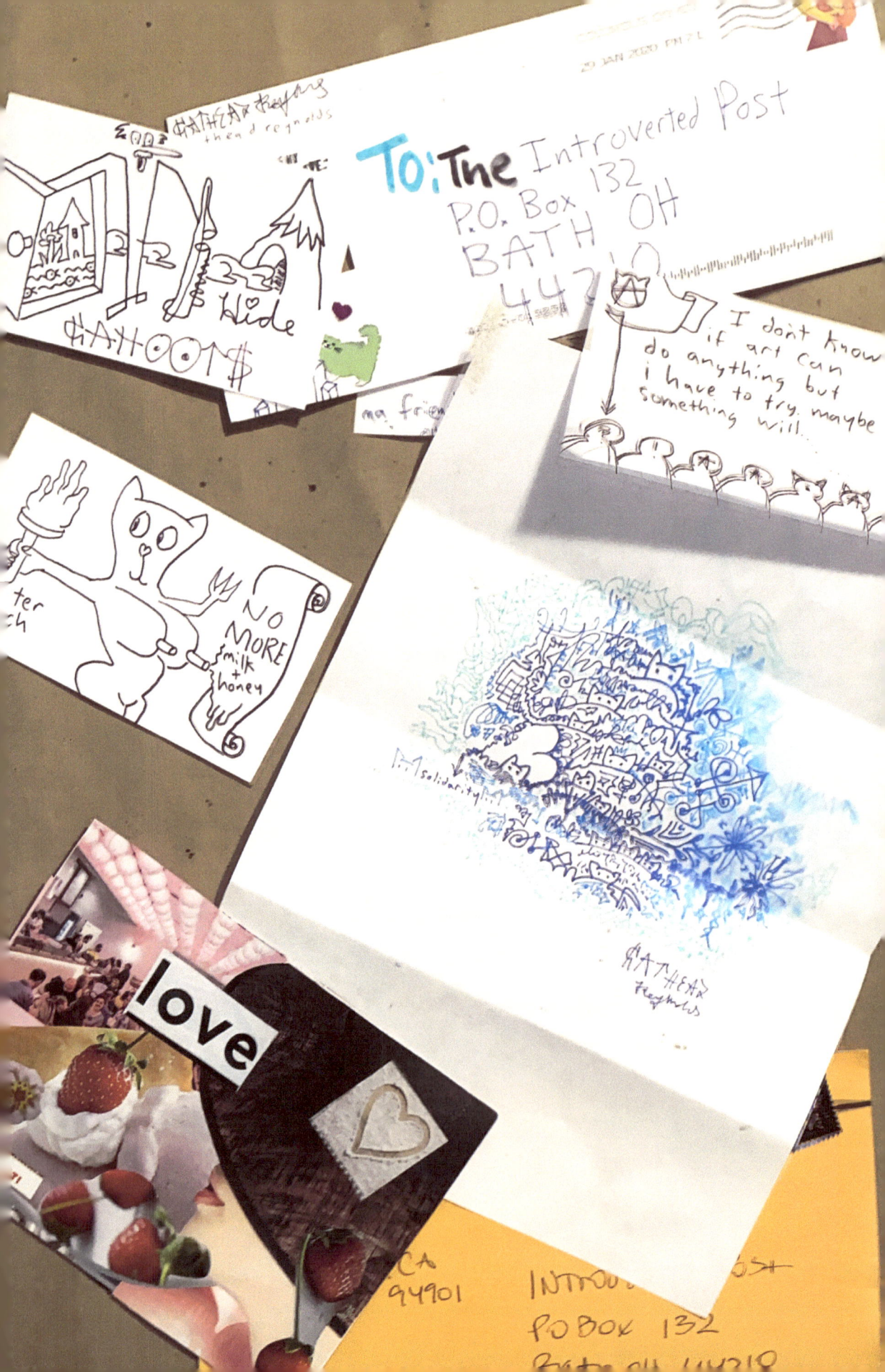

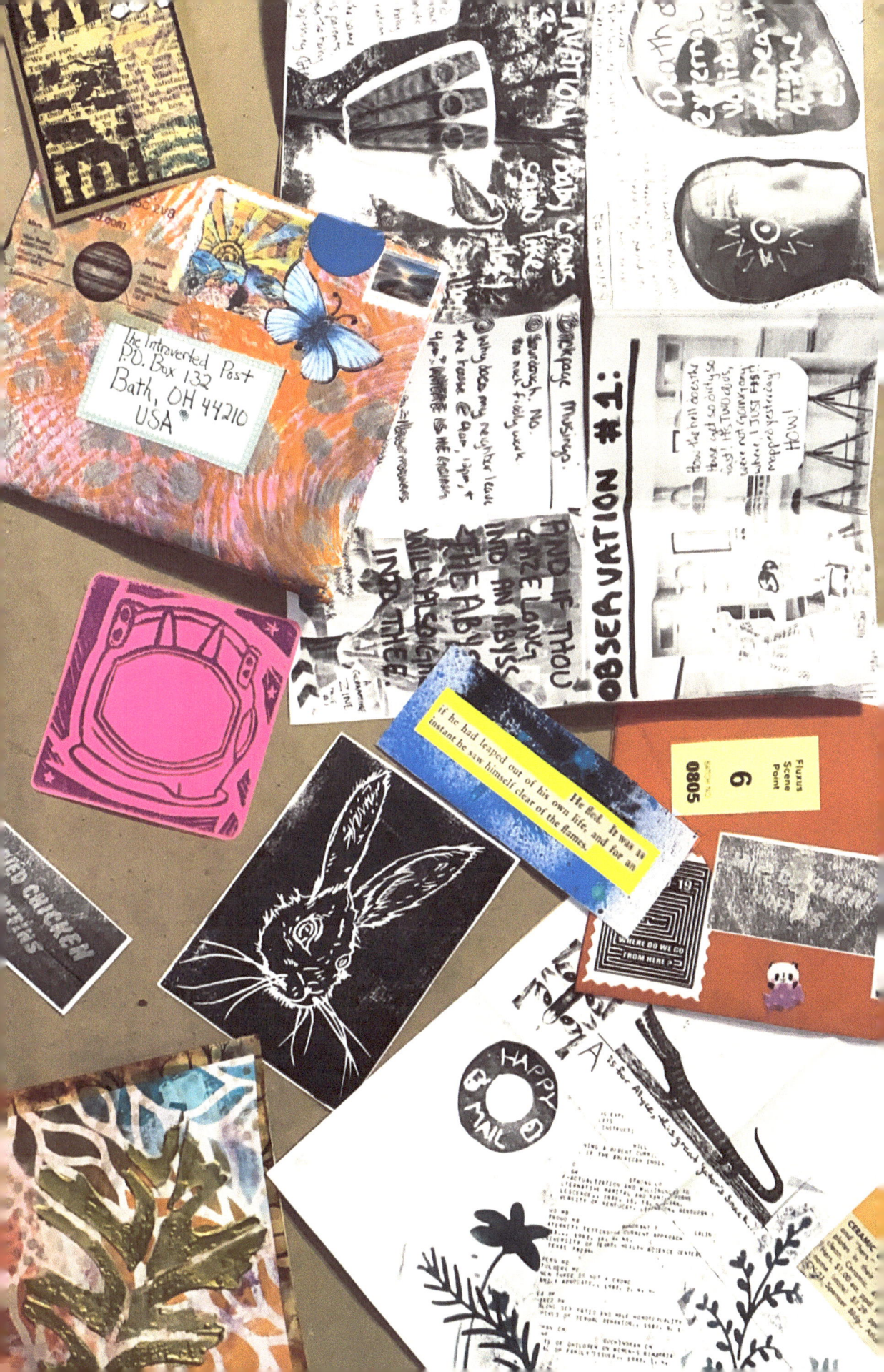

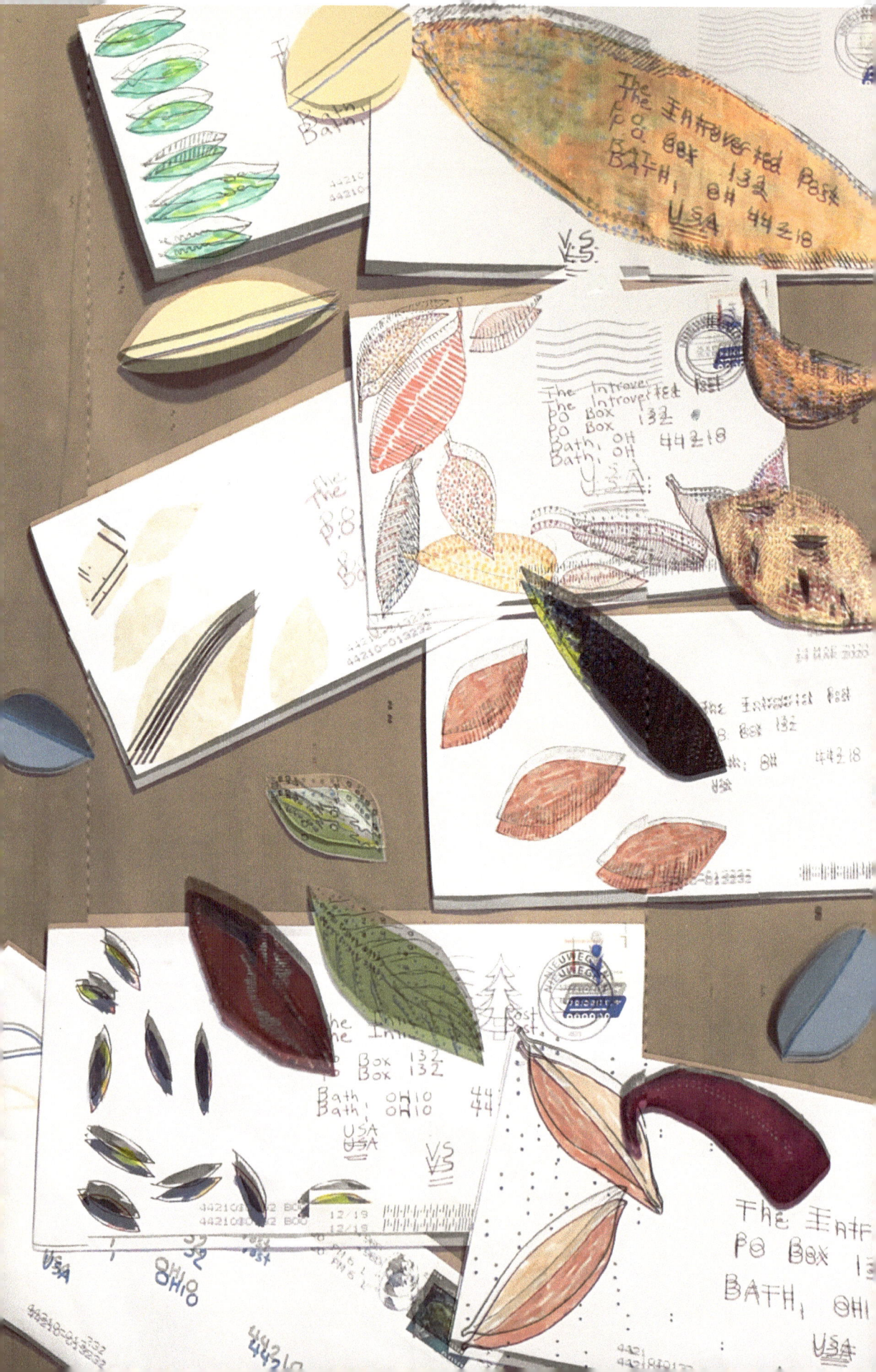

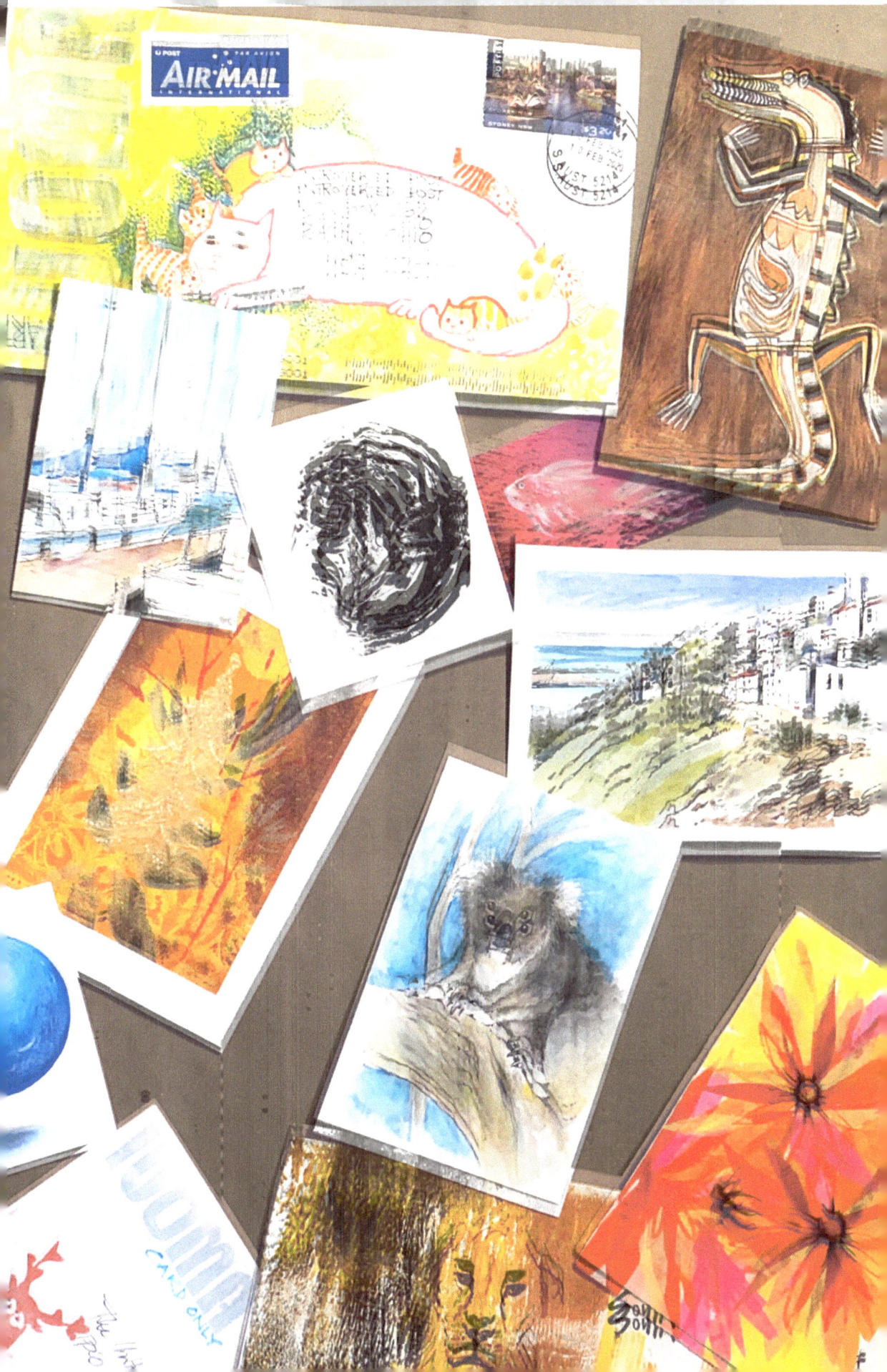

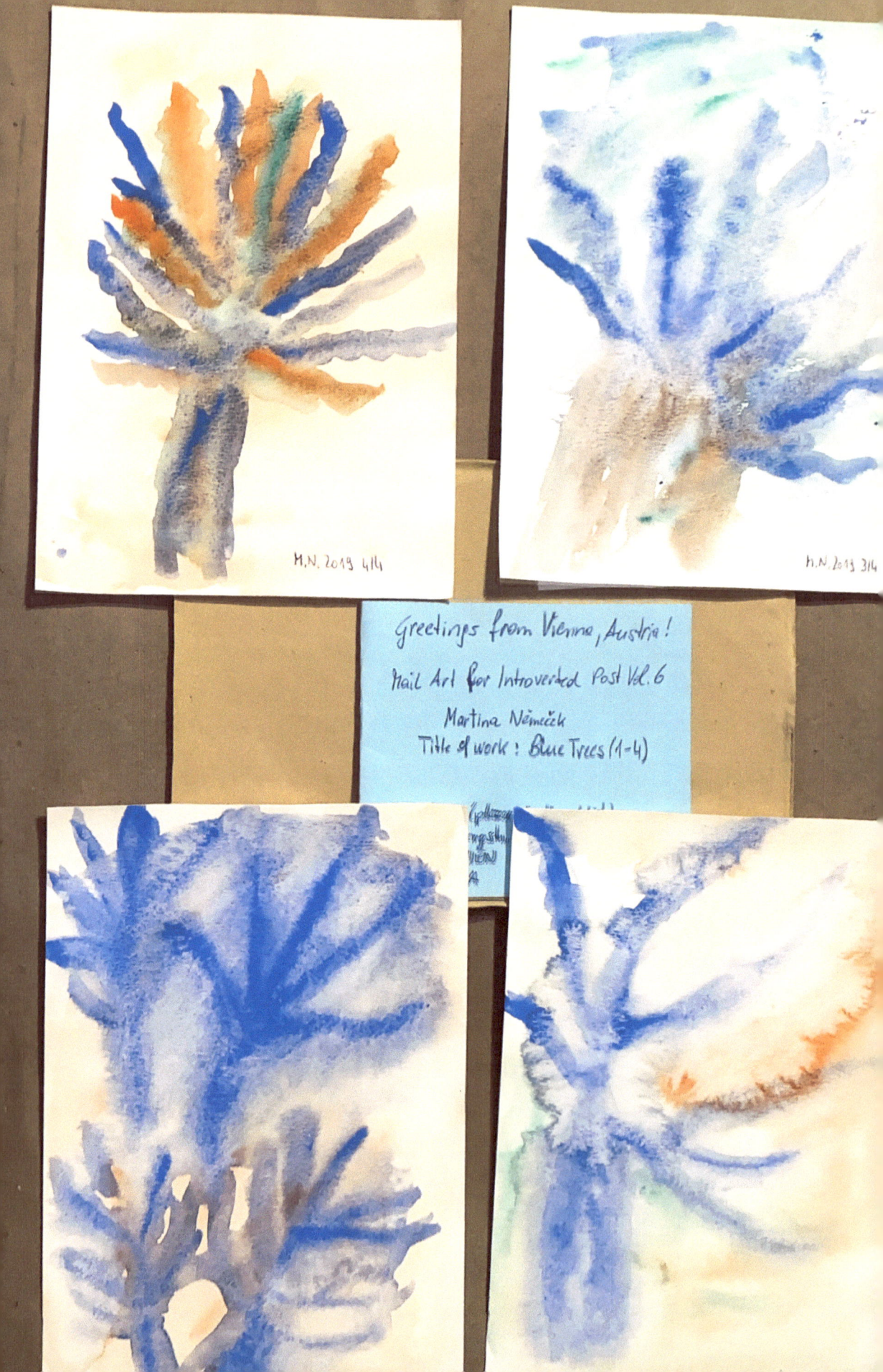

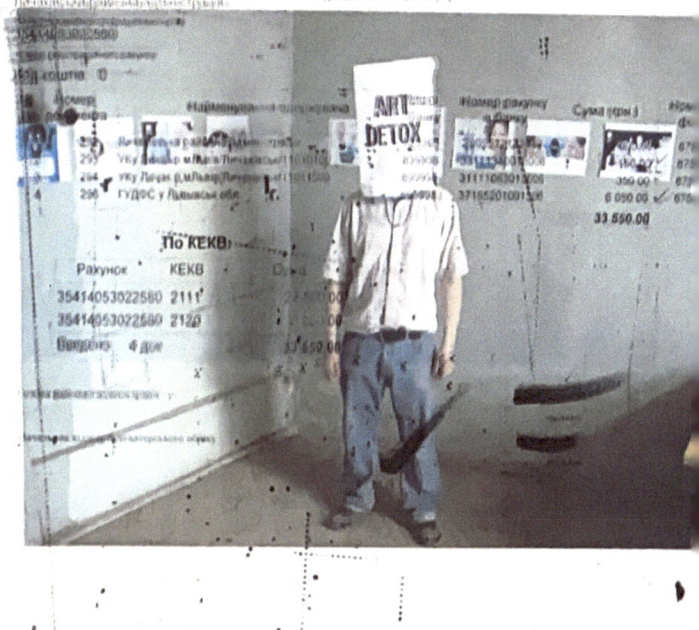
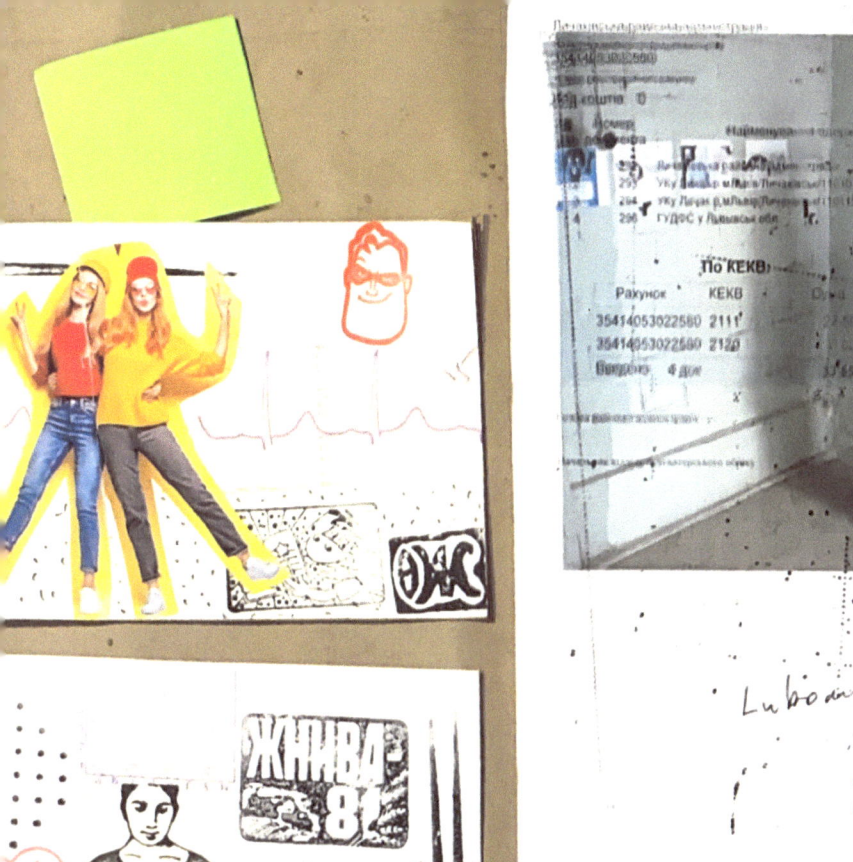

Lubomyr Tymkiv (ukraine)

EXIT TOUR

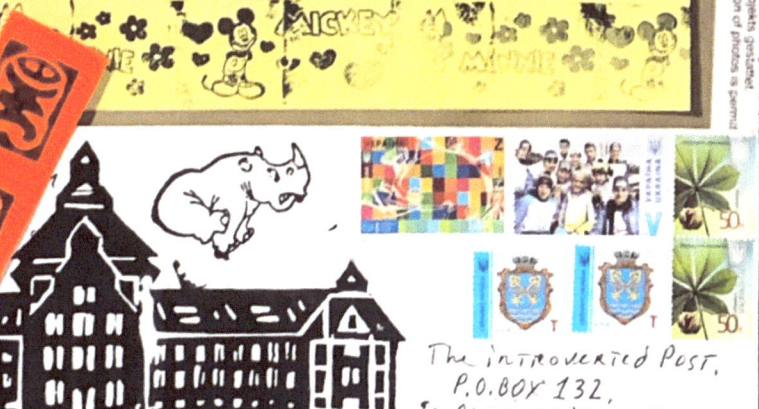

The introverted Post.
P.O. BOX 132,
BATH, OHIO,

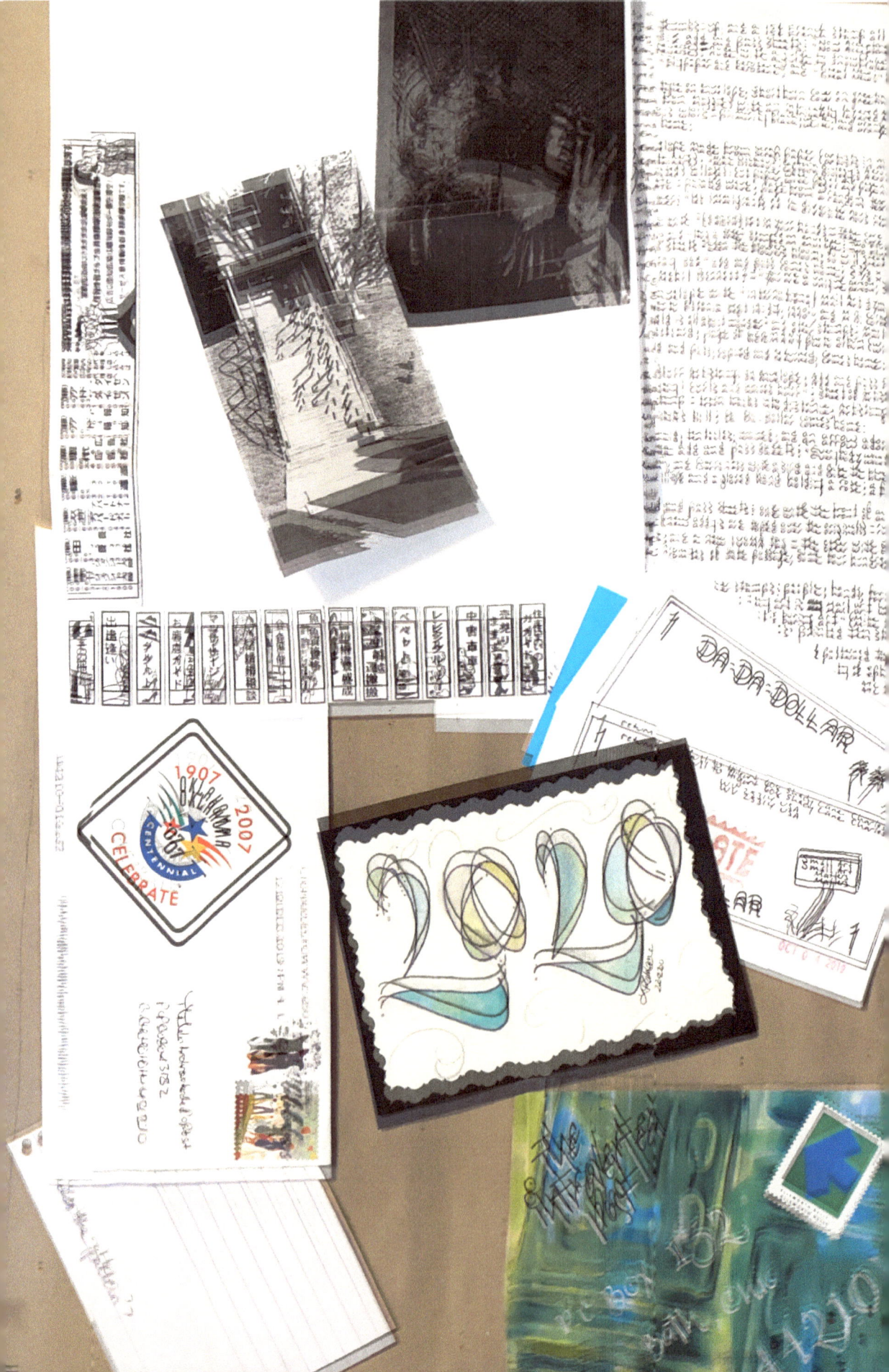

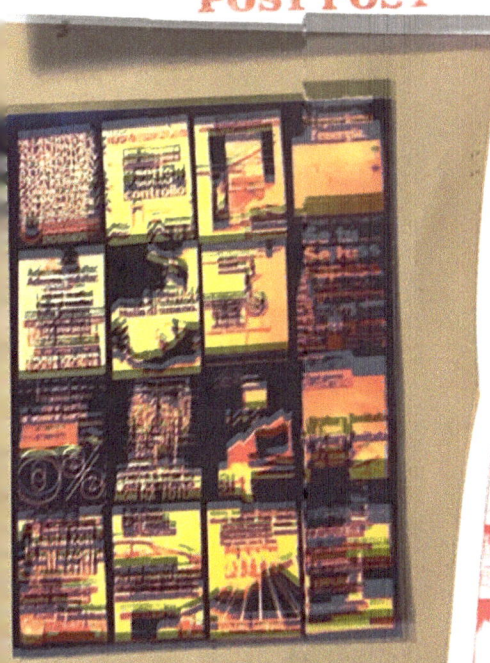

POST POST

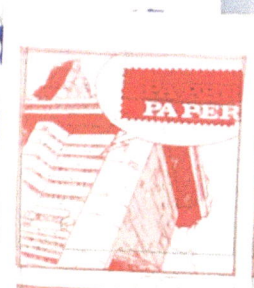
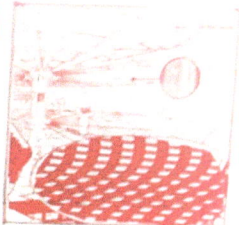
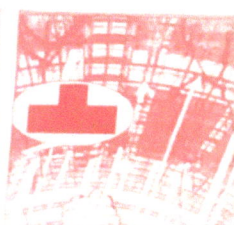
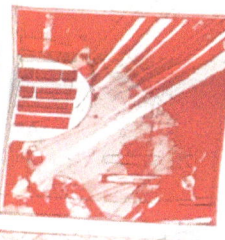
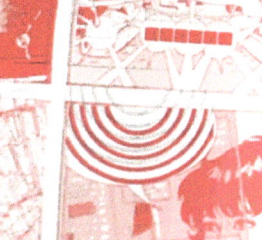
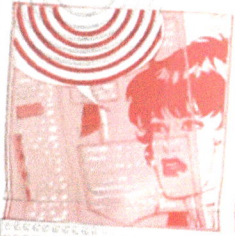
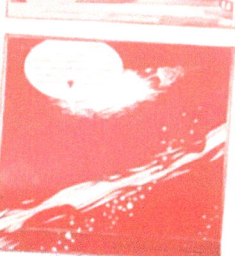

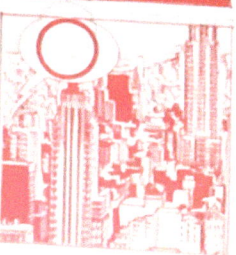

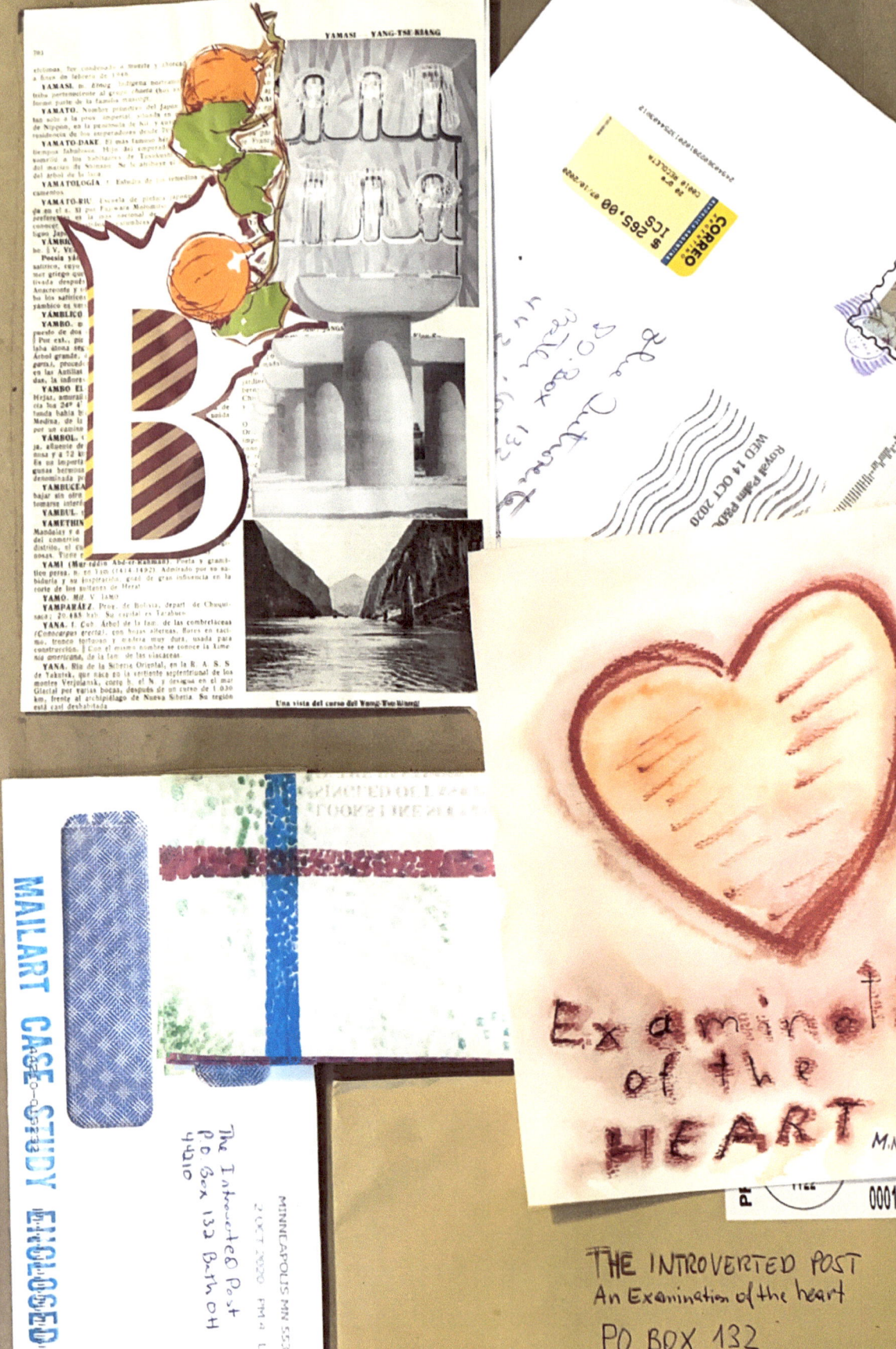

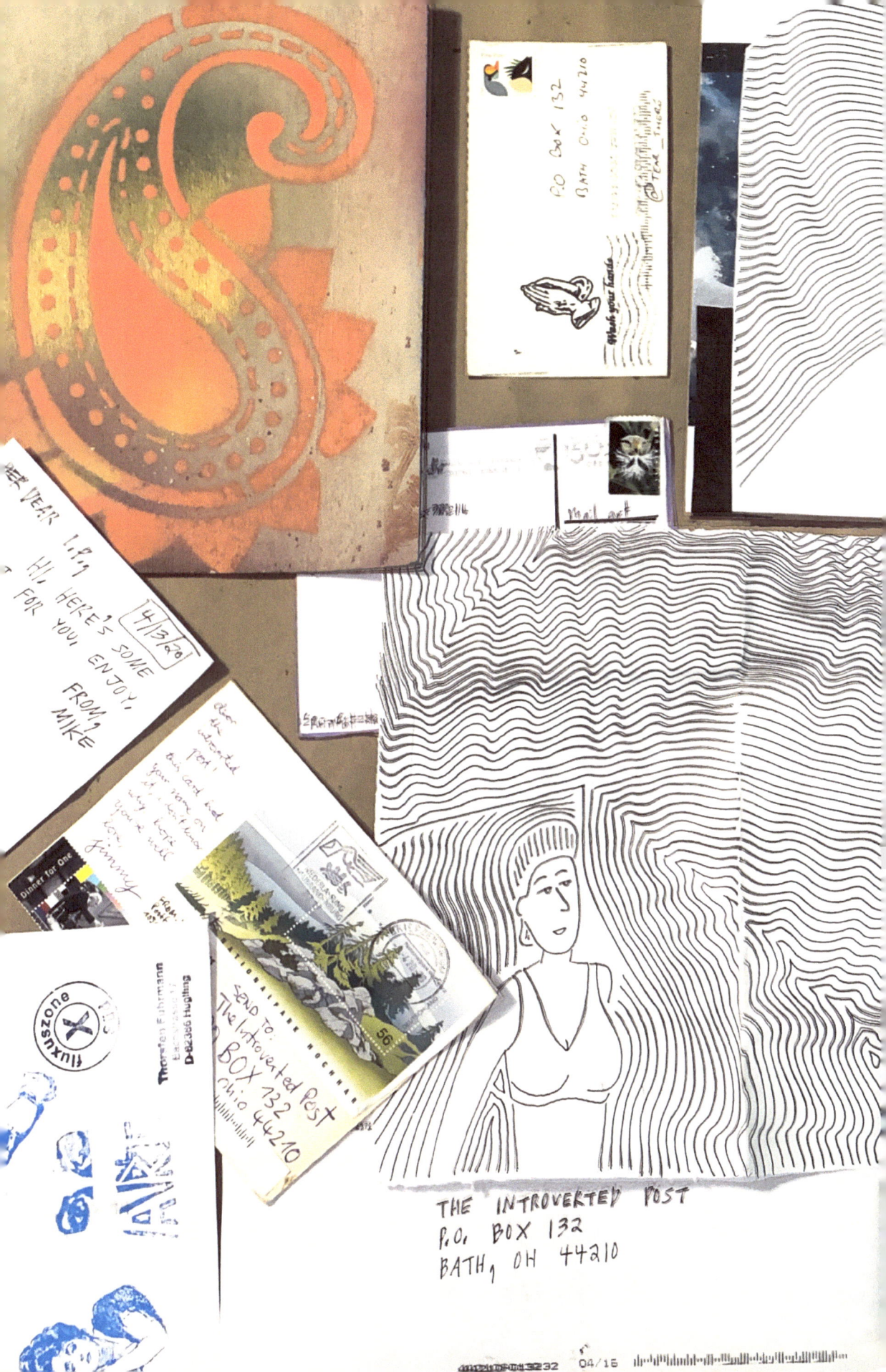

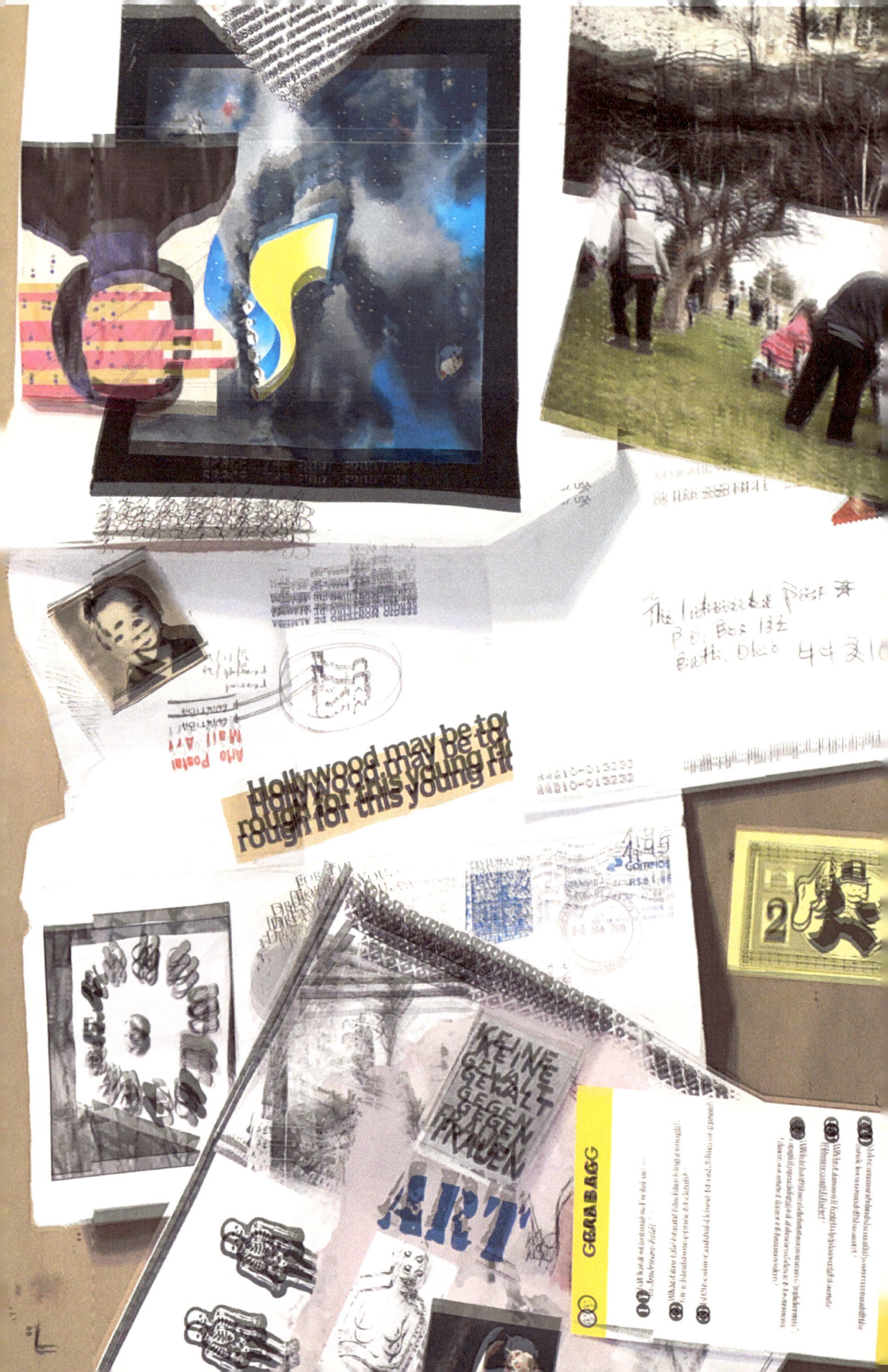

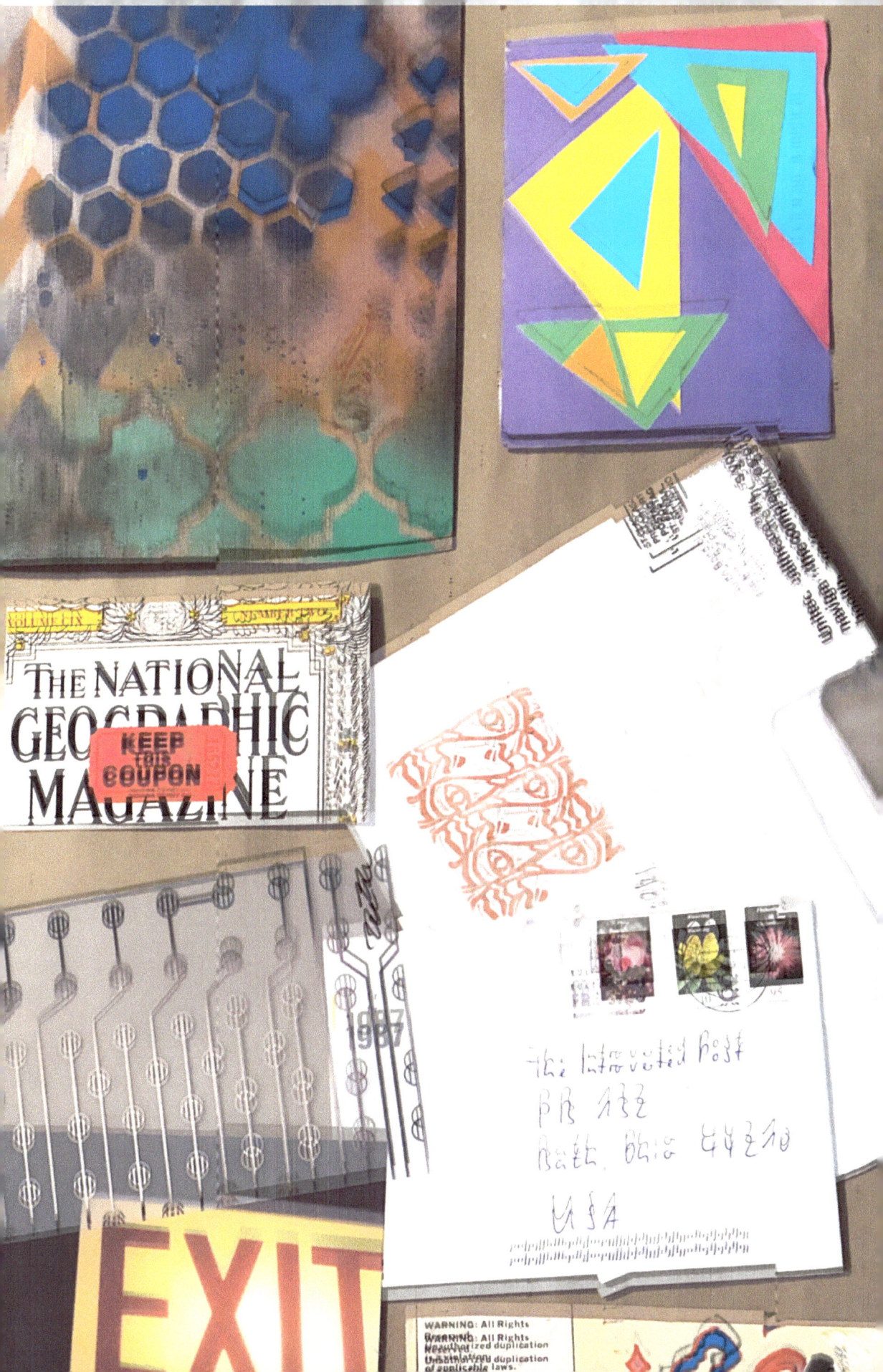

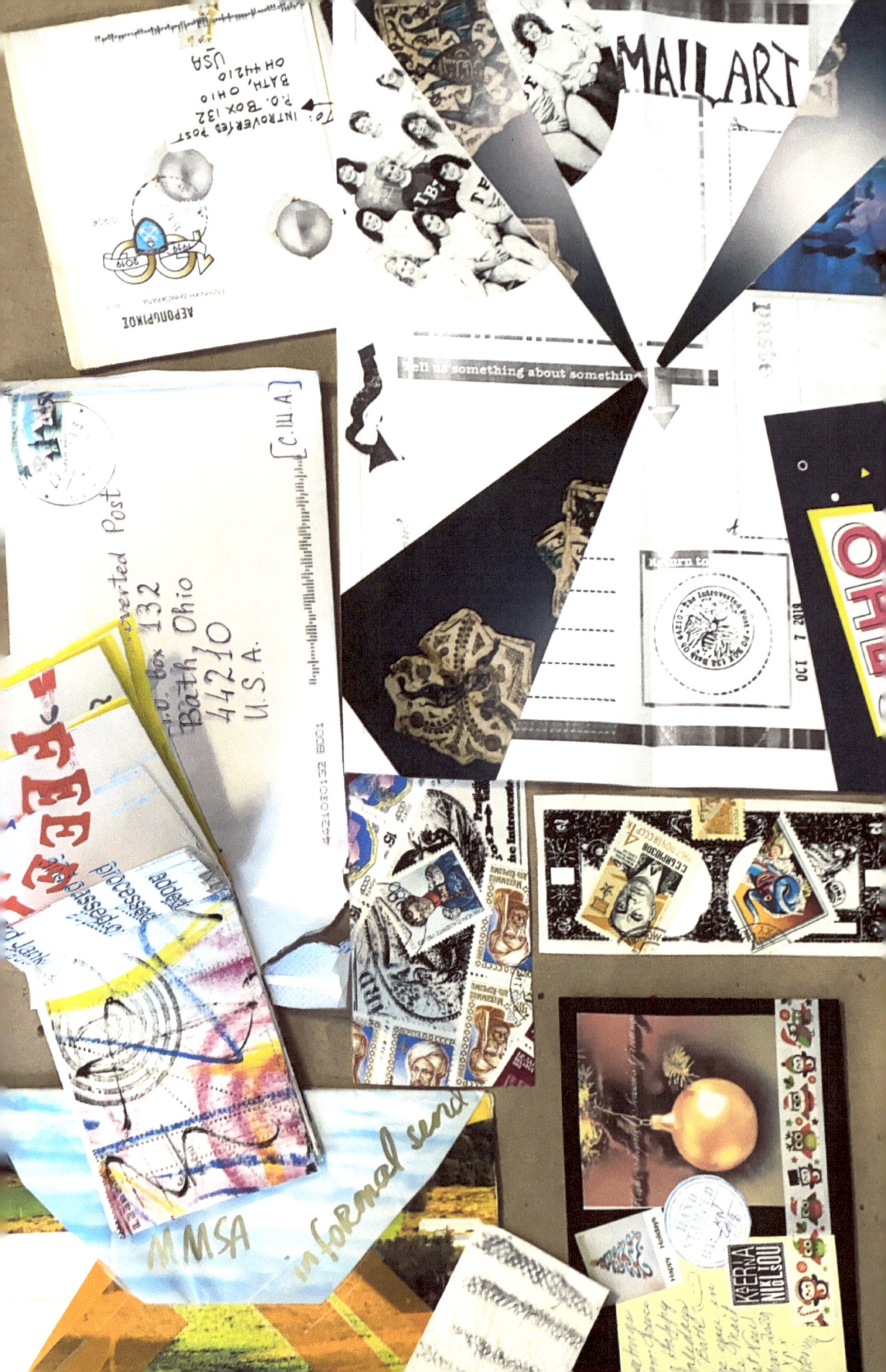

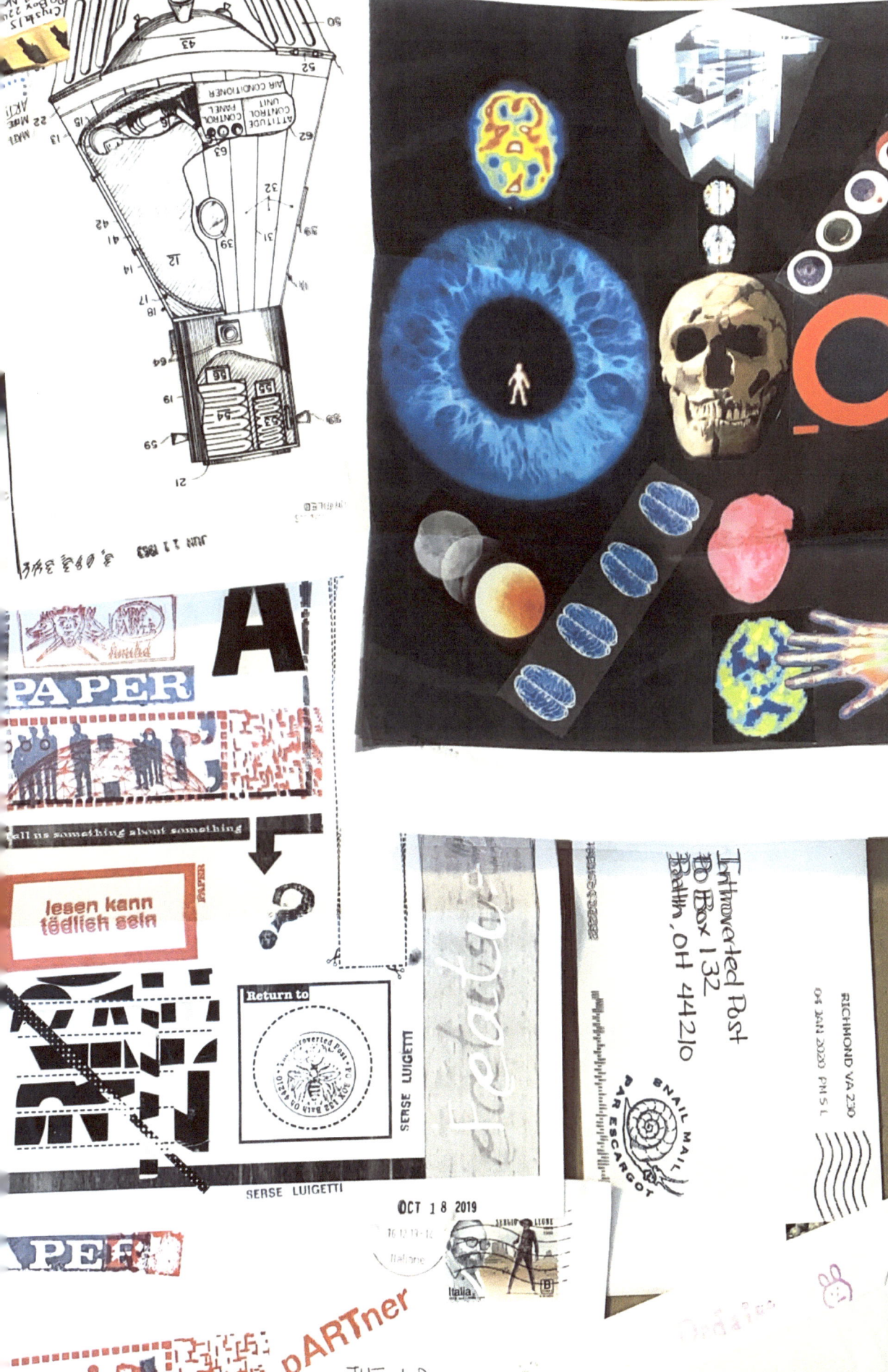

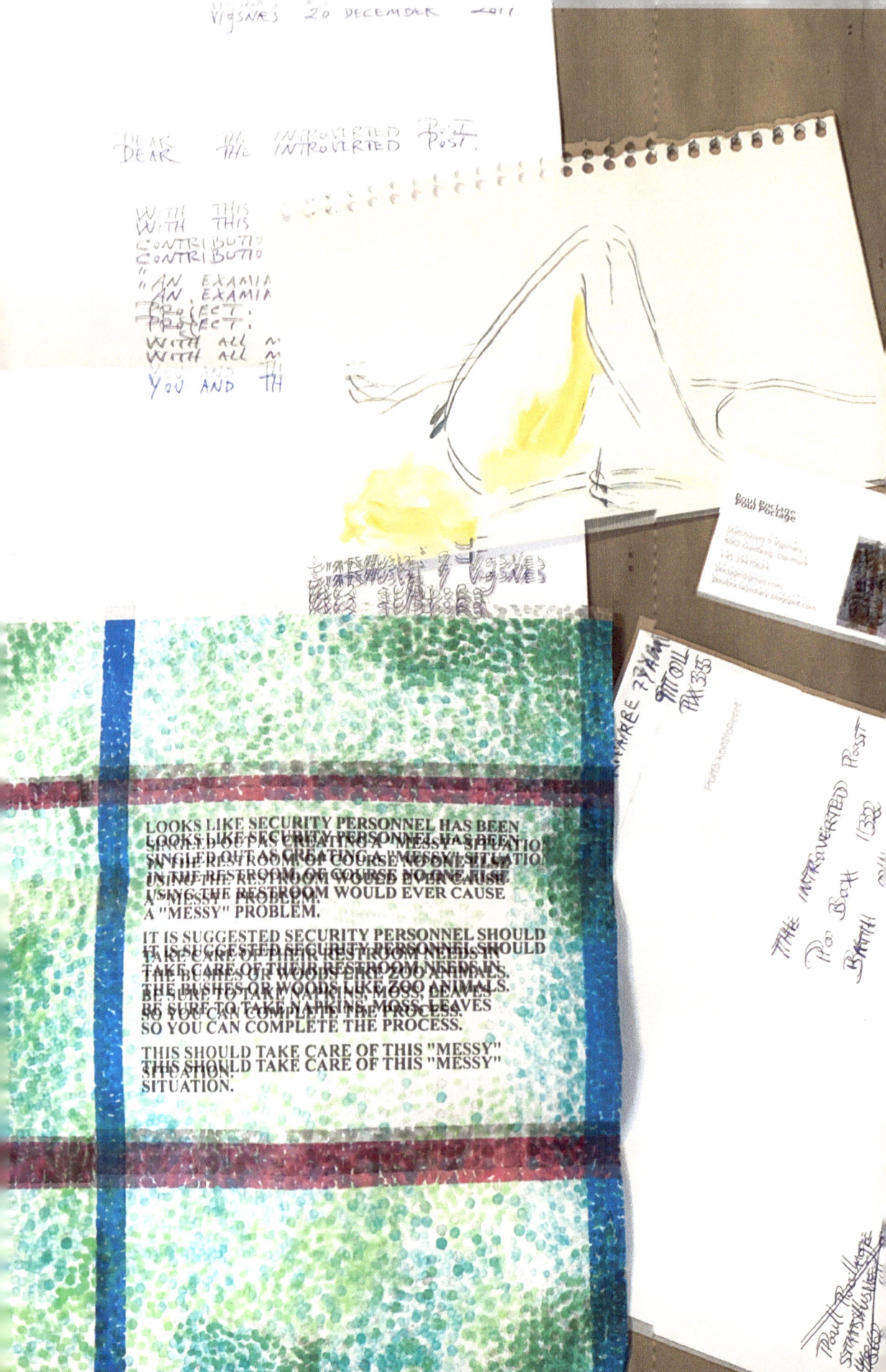

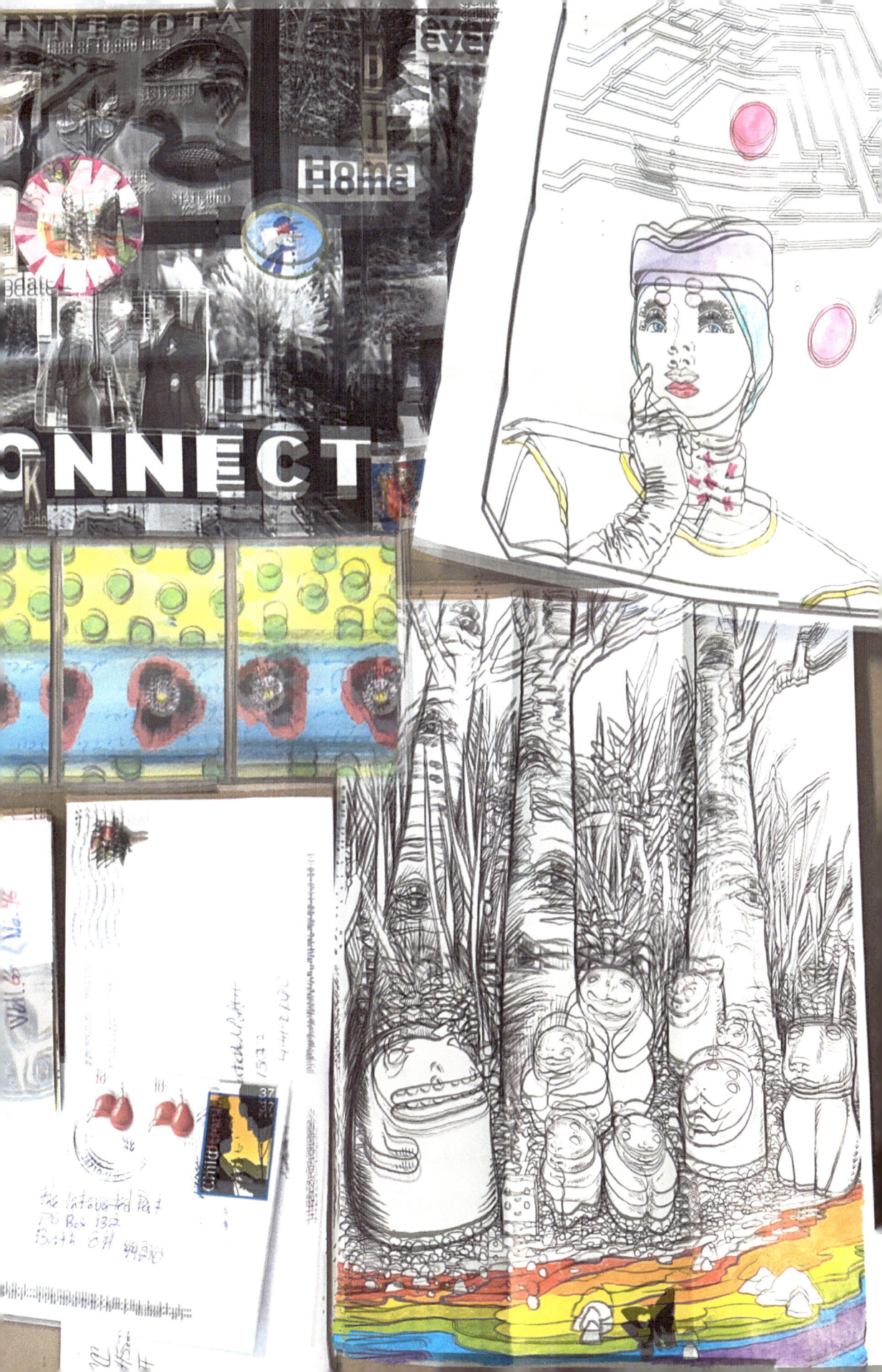

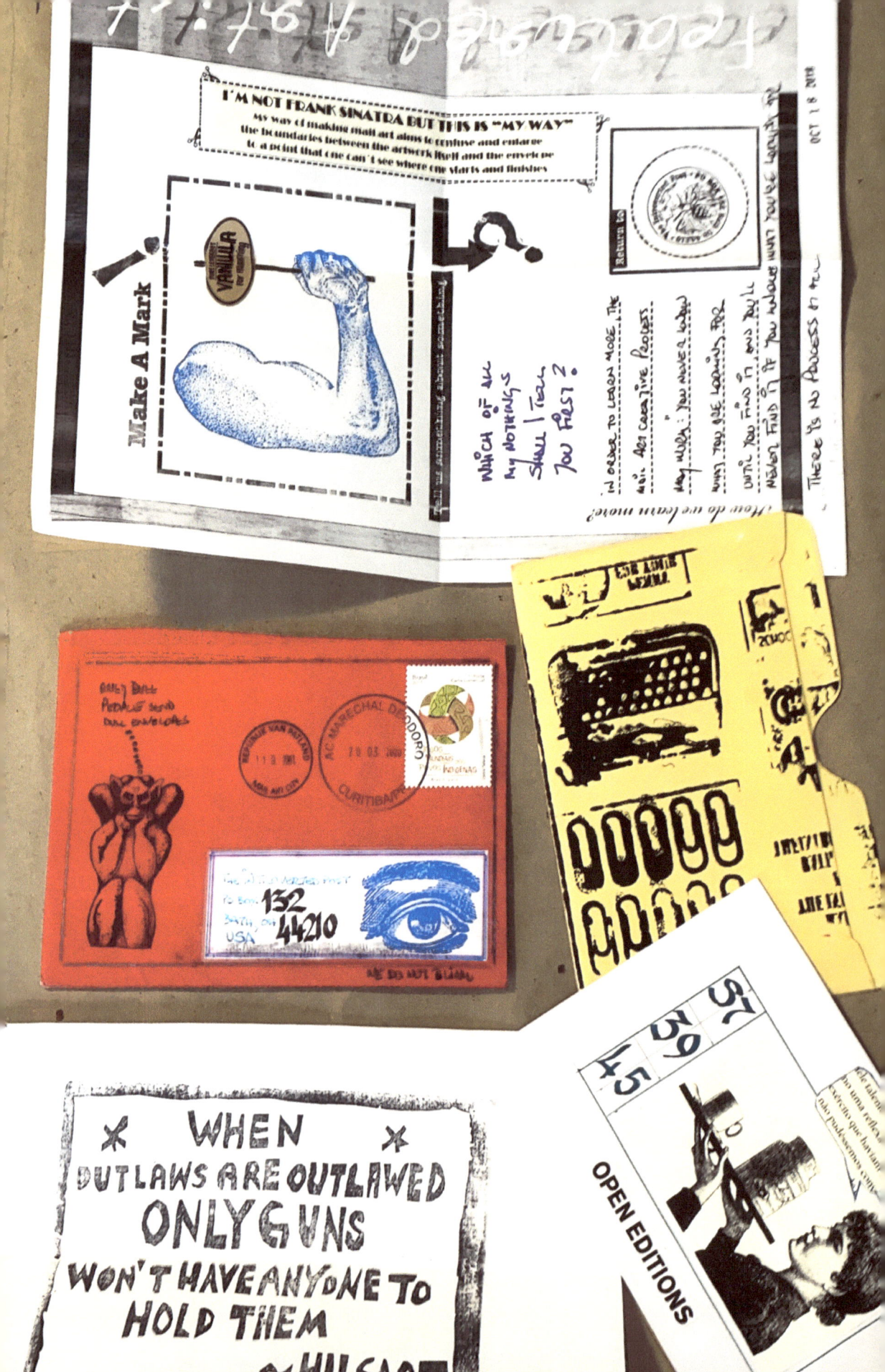

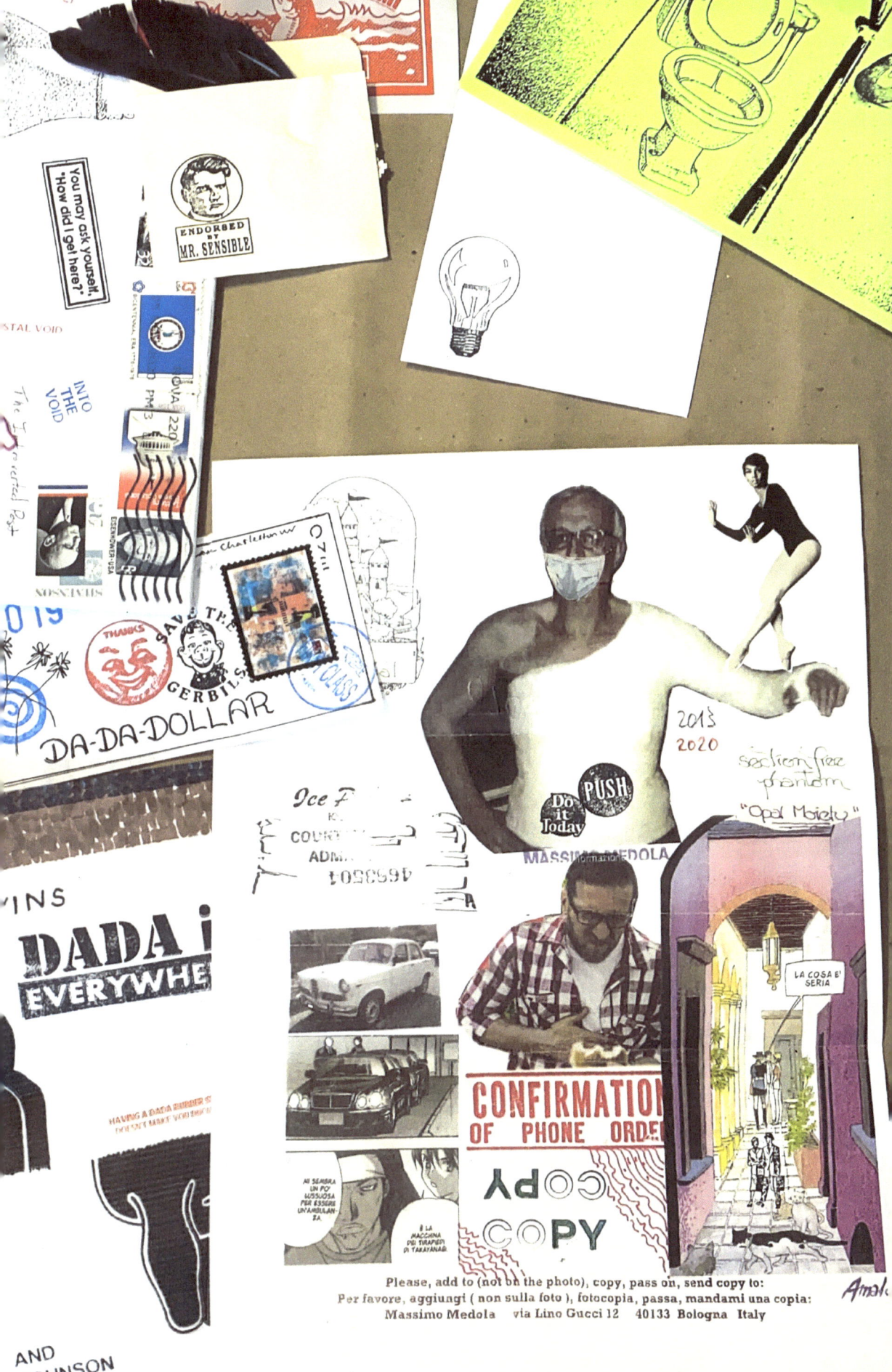

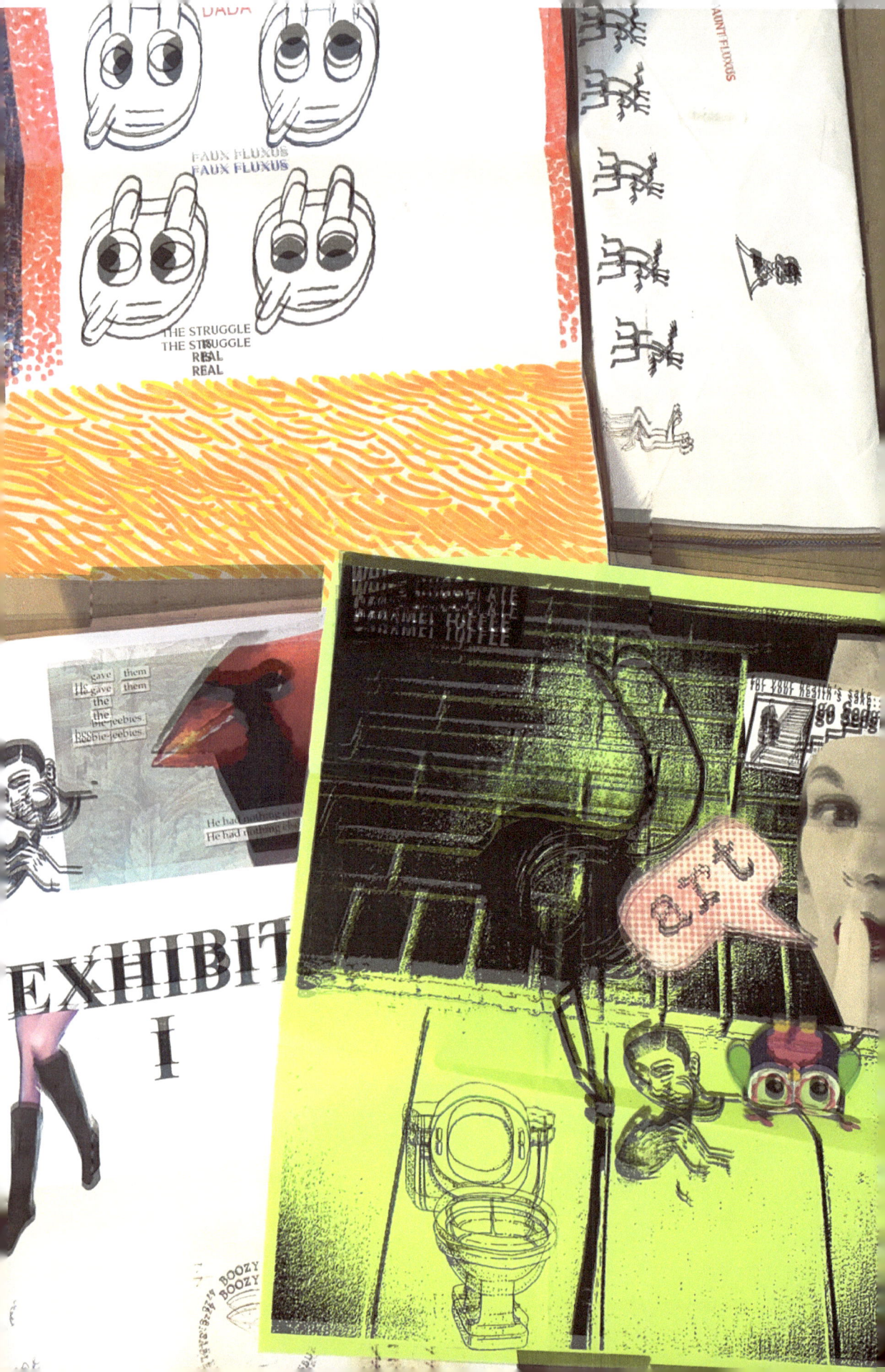

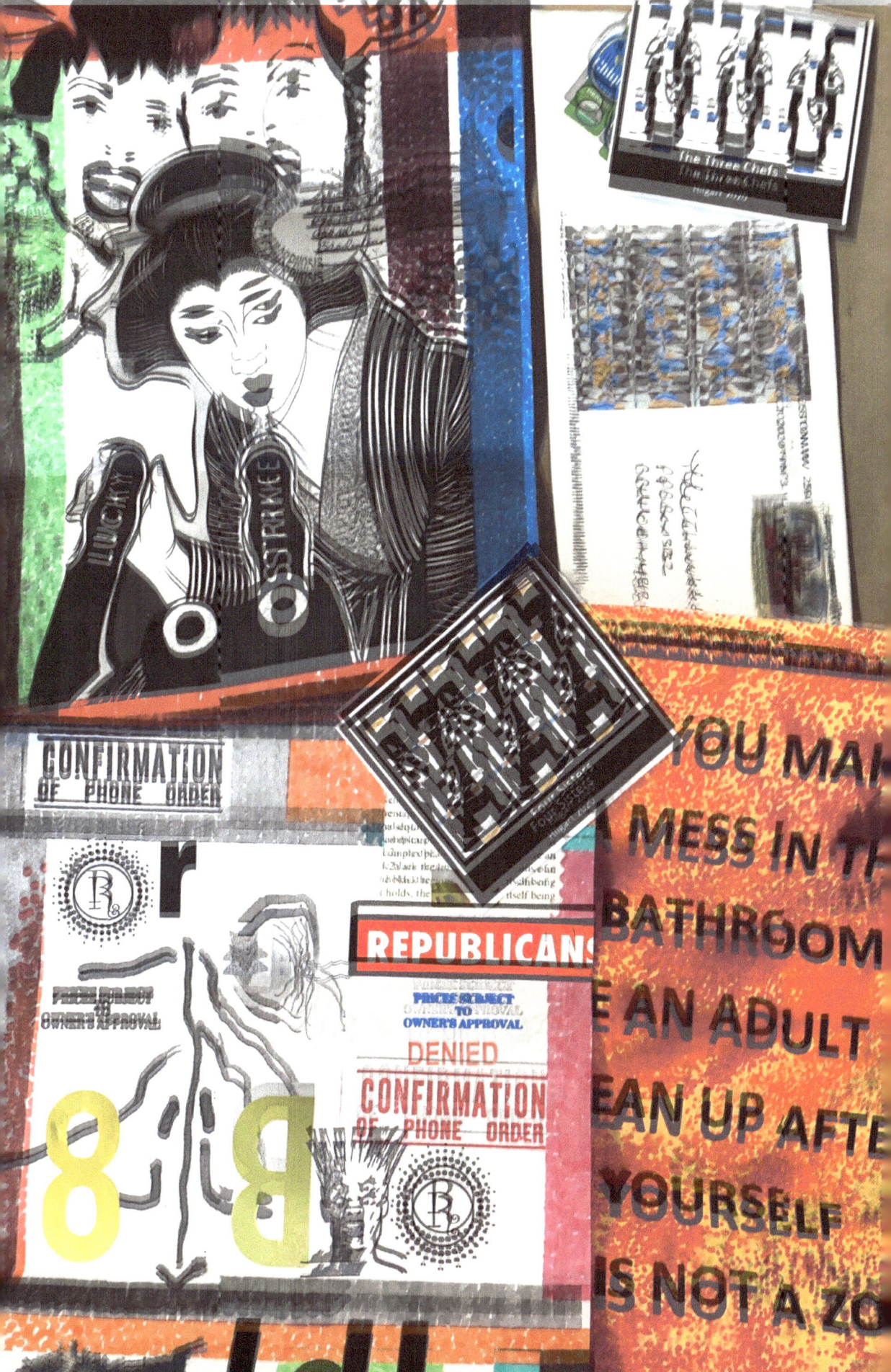

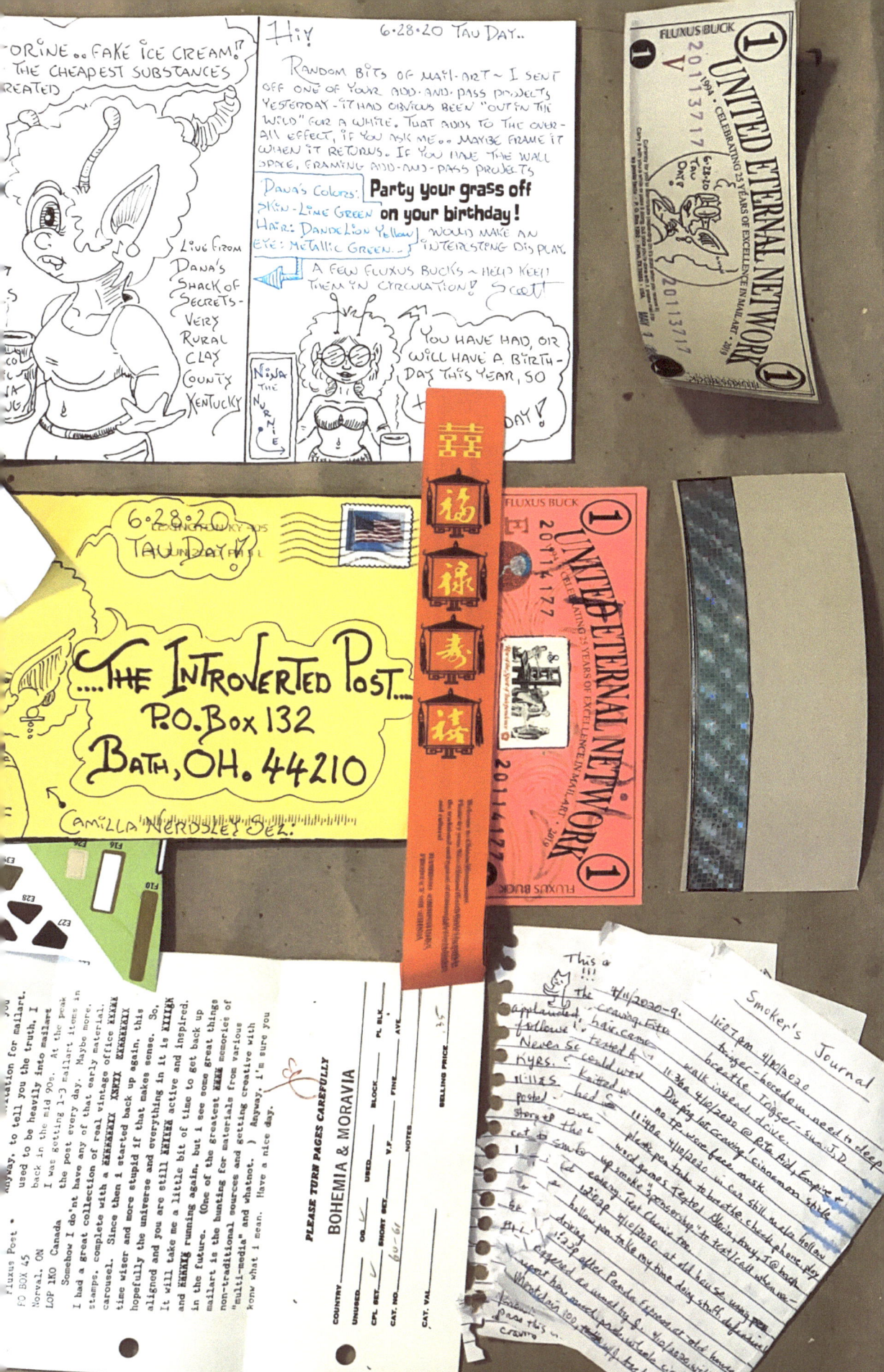

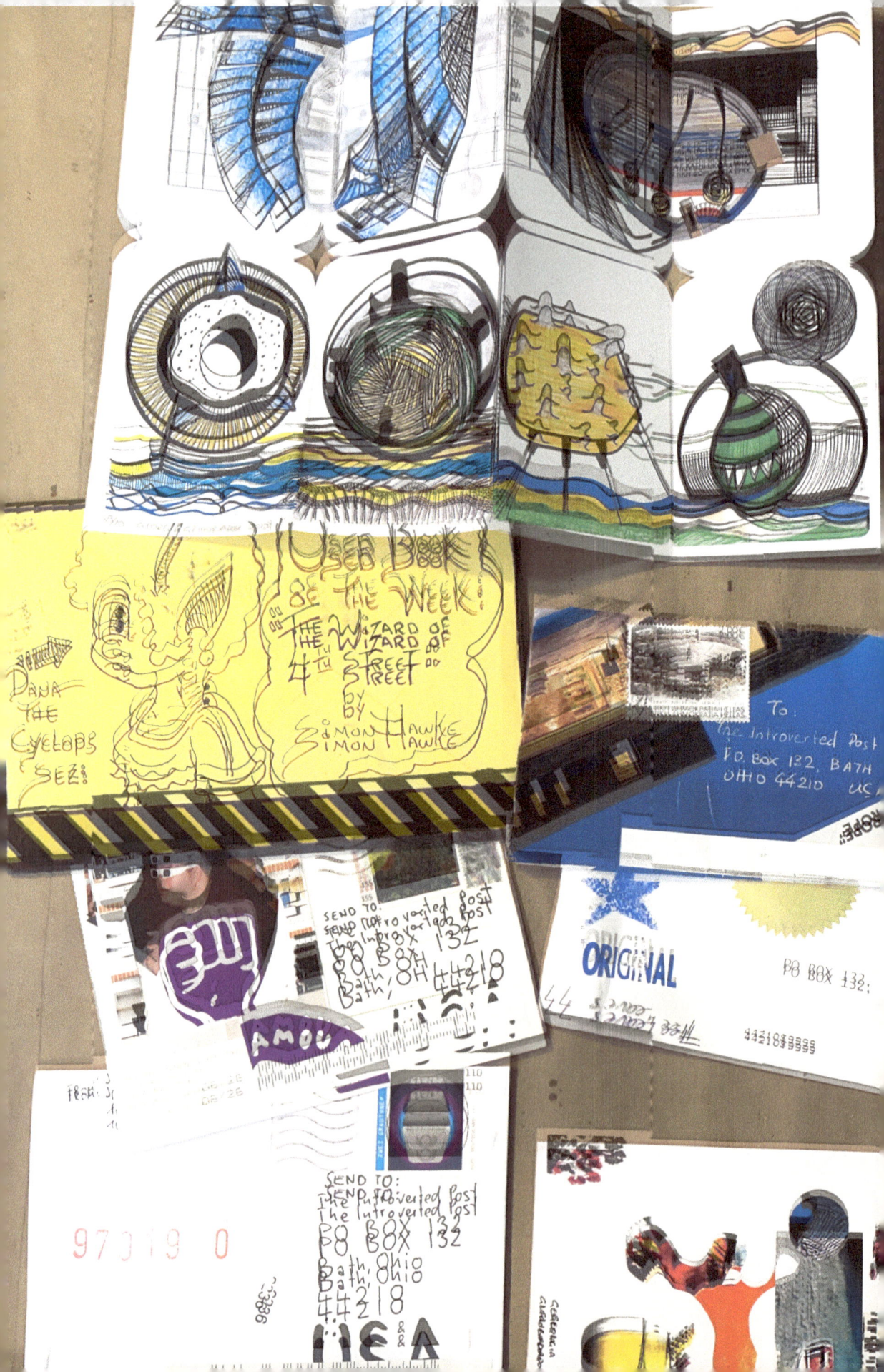

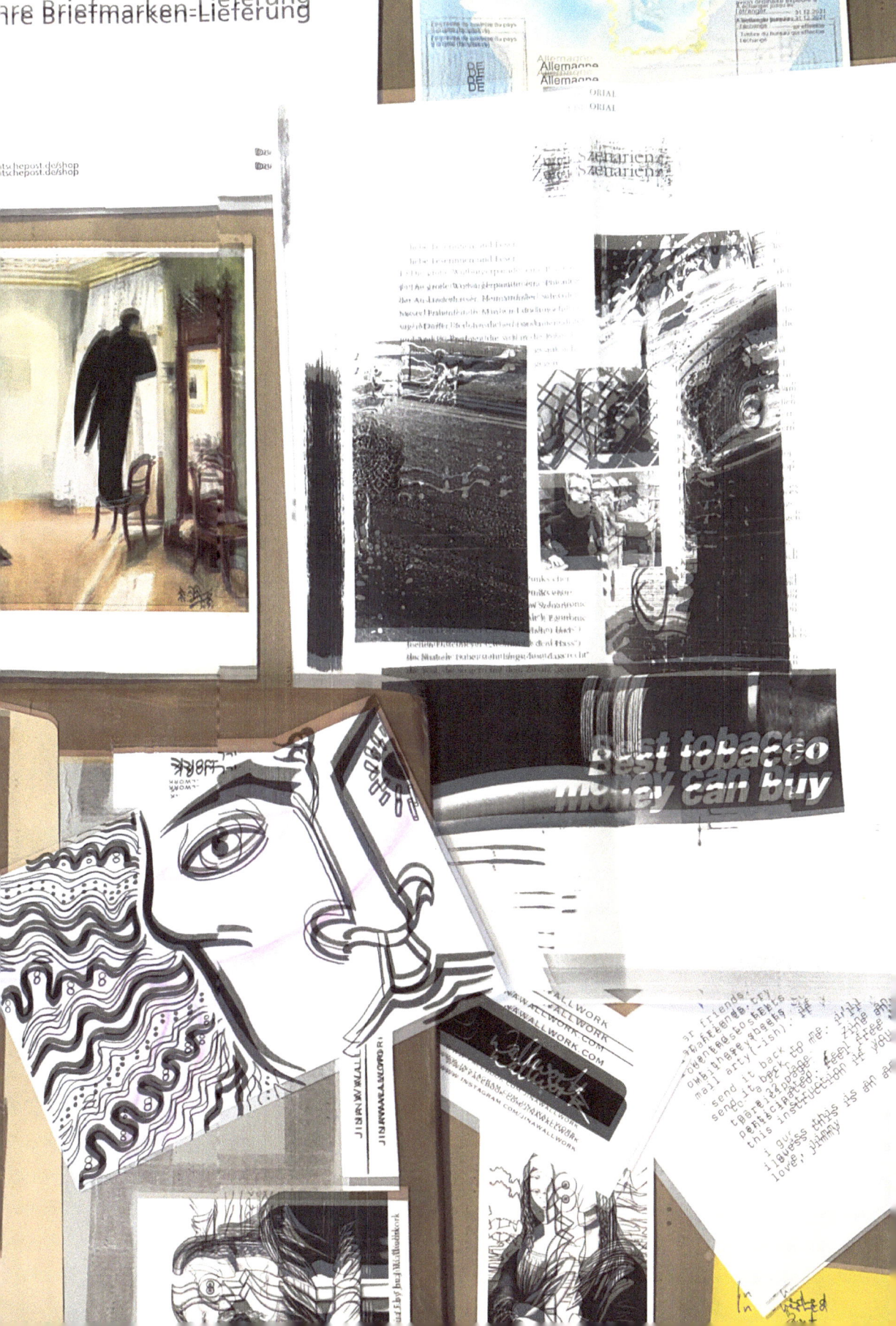

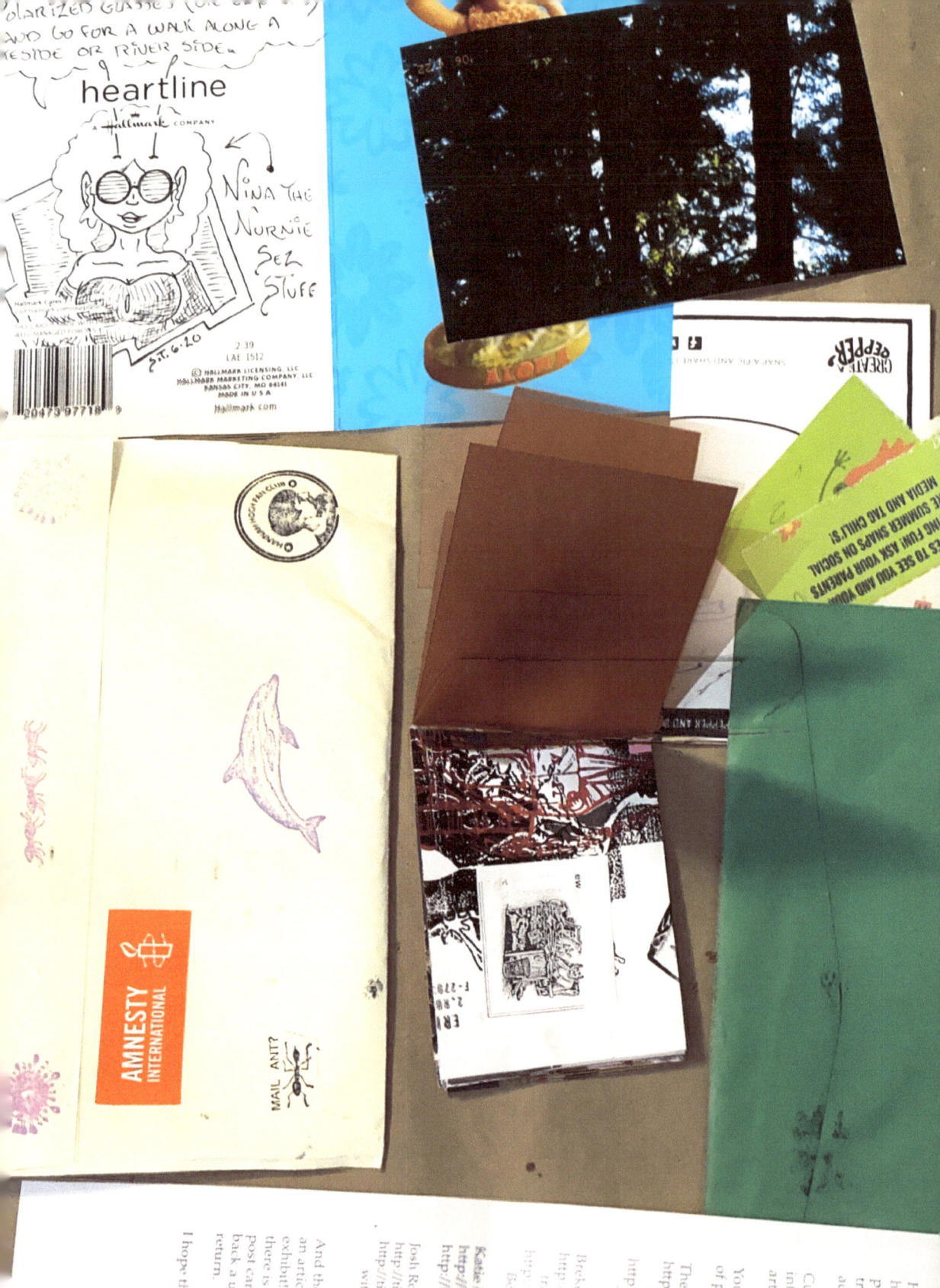

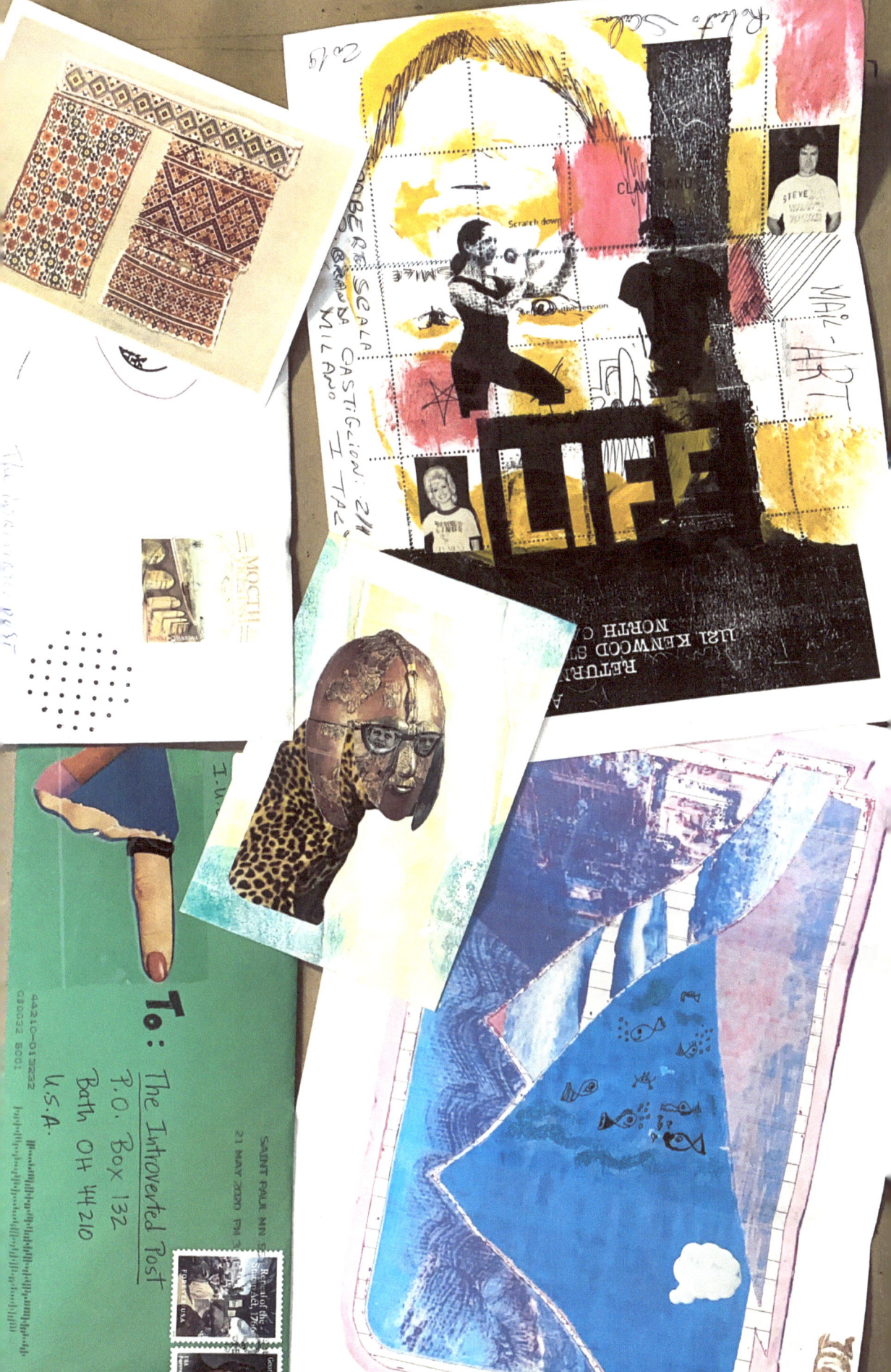

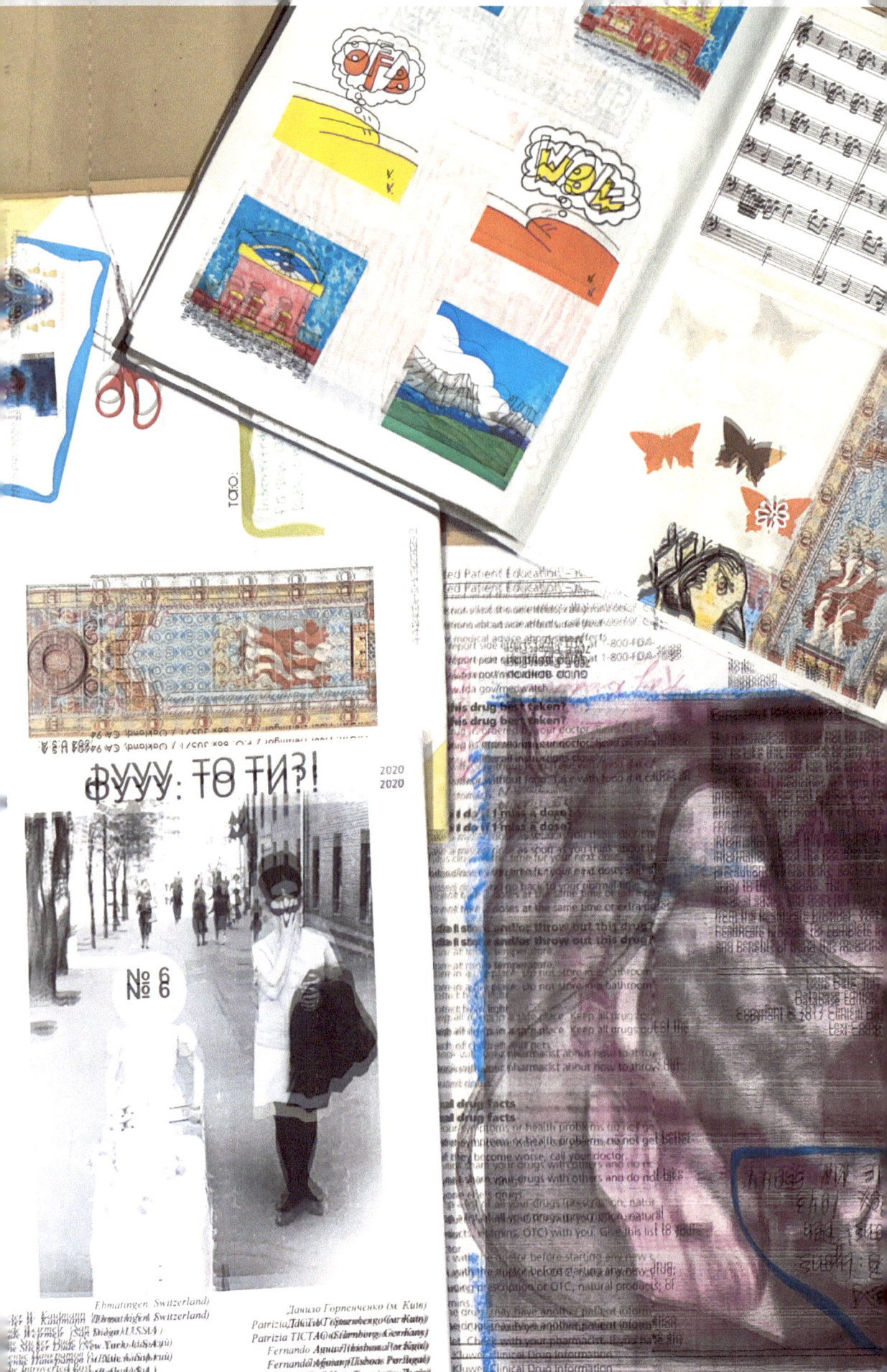

www.ingramcontent.com/pod-product-compliance
Lightning Source LLC
Chambersburg PA
CBHW051927210526
45473CB00006B/2164